May 16, 2010

A Funny Thing Happened On The Way To Enlightenment

To Dor;

one page a day
to dance life —

Love,

Kenne Hfreich

A Funny Thing Happened On The Way To Enlightenment

Lenny Ravich

Foreword by Anne Teachworth

Edited by Mackie J.V. Blanton, Ph.D.

A Publication of the Gestalt Institute Press of New Orleans/Metairie, LA USA
All Rights of English Edition are reserved to Gestalt Institute Press © Copyright 2000,
Oranit Publishers and Distributors, LTD.

Library of Congress Number:		2002093152
ISBN:	Hardcover	1-4010-6617-8
	Softcover	1-4010-6616-X

To order additional copies of this book, contact:
Xlibris.................... in the United States of America.
1-888-795-4274
www.Xlibris.com
Orders@Xlibris.com
15844-TEAC

CONTENTS

EDITOR'S NOTE

Only time and more wit will tell, but for now it seems as if Lenny Ravich is 21st-century Israel's Mark Twain or Will Rogers. Though Twain and Rogers were not psychotherapists, their witticisms were often therapeutic, like verbal salves and unguents. Though no riverboat dandy or dust bowl cowboy, Lenny's visceral wit is sheer balm to the human spirit.

The pithy observation often has that effect, rather witty or wry. In Lenny's hands, the pith is simultaneously both wry and witty—with the intent to heal. Sometimes, however, it is when the wry irony of memory stands starkly alone on the page that we can be reduced to pain and not laughter—when it is suggested to us that the origin of wit may very well be pain. An example to hand is when Lenny recalls a lesson from his mother:

> "My mother used to tell me stories almost every day. One was about the Cossacks nearly raping her, and the other was one that binds Jewish boys and their Jewish mothers into a very unusual life-script. She used to tell me about a little boy who always told his mother how much he loved her.
>
> "Years later, when he became a young bachelor, he met a girl and proposed marriage. She said she would marry him only on one condition. He must take a knife, go home, cut his mother's heart out, and bring the heart to her. That way, the girl would be sure that he truly loved her. So the young

man bought a dagger, went home and cut his mother's heart out.

"With his mother's still beating heart in hand, he hurried to his future bride. On the way, he stumbled and fell. It was then that he heard the heart murmur softly to him, 'Be careful, my son. Don't hurt yourself. Are you all right?'

"I later discovered that other Jewish mothers told their young Jewish sons the same story."

This recollection forces me to wonder how well we really know someone else, if we don't also know his painful experiences, even when we believe that we know him enough to first-name him, as I do in this, my editor's note. Never mind that Lenny makes us chuckle or laugh again soon after we have read this recollection—because, nonetheless, we just can't forget it. Will we ever be able to?

It is precisely pain itself that requires laughter. What I find fascinating about Lenny is that his sense for the humorous—as he tells it—did not arise after pain—unless birth itself is pain for some newborns—but before it, as if it were co-conceived with him embryonicly. Hence, humor was born with him—from the same womb. Ironicly, therefore, his mother simultaneously gave birth to him and to his sense for the humorous.

It is not illogical for us to assume an association between humor and the body. Just as Lenny began this life in a body, mankind has always associated humor with the body. Of course, some of us will—won't we?—recall that humour/humor etymologically comes into Middle English (1150-1475) from the Latin *(h)ûmôr*, which is derived, in turn, from Latin for to be wet *(ûmçre)*. Hence, the original English sense of the term included a reference to bodily fluids and, consequently, became a medical term during Europe's Middle Ages for diagnosing the relative health of a person. So one could determine the mental condition of a person by referring to "the humours" of the body's blood, phlegm, black bile, or yellow bile.

Therefore, historically speaking, though the modern sense of the term suggests possessing a comic quality for perceiving and causing bemusement in others, humor etymologically suggests possessing a mental disposition or frame of mind for spying out the capricious and freakish in others. So, generally speaking, the person who possesses a sharp sense of humor is gifted principally with recognizing and expressing incongruities and peculiarities in human behavior.

"In order to be funny, I think that a person has to have had a screwed up childhood," Lenny observes. Otherwise, how can one "see humor and paradox as ways to deal with the misery?"

It is not so easy to categorize Lenny's work. Is it a personal memoir, a semi-fictionalized autobiography, a run-on script for stand-up comics, a codex of droll life lessons? However one might classify it, one thing that I find intriguing about Lenny's work is that though he seems to teach from the male point of view, he seems to have learned life's lessons primarily from the female—his mother, his sister, his wife, his therapist, his colleague. He hardly ever seems connected to the male as teacher, unless he encounters them in books. So he quotes males but creates strong portraiture of women. He mentions his father but once, obliquely suggesting that his father taught him to discern life in a joke.

> "I was sad when he died, and joyful. A load was lifted from my shoulders. He was a man full of mirth, smiles, and rage. He was the one who taught me how to make peroxide when I was seven years old.
>
> "'You take a little peroxide and mix it with more peroxide, and—wham!—you've got peroxide!' he instructed me often.
>
> "That was a lovely first joke to a young kid.
>
> "It was even lovelier to have come from my father."

However, one of the strongest moments in this work is when he captures the origin of female anger.

> "Seemingly, women are allowed all feelings available, *except her very own anger*. That's why many women cry when they get mad. God forbid a woman should express her

anger. Then she's considered either a 'controlling bitch' ('She always cries and bawls to get me to do things her way!') or, at best, a "mindless puppy" ('Ahh, you're so cute when you get angry'.). In either case, words are the man's weapons of destruction."

The droll and the sad, on the other hand, are the least of the thrust and sense of this work. It's Lenny's style of delivery that captivates us in these pages. We have the sense that we are being entertained from the stage of Life—stage center—by a stand-up, picaresque American émigré to Israel who is unquestionably the composite gestalt of the comic, the actor, the teacher, the psychotherapist.

It will be difficult for me to suggest what makes for such a composite in a single individual. What I can suggest, however, is that what makes such an individual persist—what makes him insist on sustaining this composite persona—is the student, the student that each of us possesses within. Because Lenny is able to discern the potential student in others, the attraction for him to take center stage in his composite persona resonates with our underlying need for the comic, actor, teacher, and psychotherapist. In Lenny, we get them all at once.

Lenny loves the student in us. We see this in his treatment of his own high school pupils whom he taught in Israel: "I [always showed] them respect, of course—for where they were, and not where they should be. By my treating every kid as if he/she were a 'little professor'."

Not a little teacher, but a little professor.

I believe that he discerns in all of us the latent potential and the subconscious desire for the highest of achieved personae; that is, our potential and desire to be a teacher of teachers to and for others, even in the smallest of ways.

When the student (talmid) within is ready, the teacher (rebbe) within will show up.

As readers, we measure our task of having something ourselves to contribute against the challenge that the originality of an author's genius brings to bear. We can each do Leonard Ravich a good deal of justice by contributing our own intimate talmidic readership to this work, and by having our own rebbe within recommend it to others.

Mackie Blanton

FOREWORD

When I was growing up, I was often confused by conflicting messages from the grownups: "You're taking this way too seriously," they'd say one day and then, "You don't take things seriously enough," the next. I was often warned, "Wait, you'll see. You won't be able to laugh things off when you grow up!" Thus, taking things seriously became synonymous with maturity, responsibility and dealing with reality. Laughing things off was synonymous with immaturity, irresponsibility, and the avoidance of reality.

Then along came Norman Cousins, who refused to deal seriously with his rather depressing reality. Instead of waiting to die as he was told to do, he got the bright idea to rent some comedy films and take his mind off his fate. In his book, *Anatomy of an Illness*, he described how laughing improved his physical health so much that it chased his terminal illness away. To the amazement of his doctors, Cousins not only outlived his prognosis but, as they say, he lived to laugh about it long after some of his doctors had died.

He proved that laughter had more of a positive influence on physical health than anyone ever knew before.

Lenny Ravich has applied the same approach within the often much-too-serious arena of mental health. He refuses to make himself feel bad by taking serious things more seriously. That's a tall order for someone living in Israel. Effective solutions to dealing with reality are hard to come by there. "What else can I do? I might as well laugh," Lenny muses. "At least it keeps me in a good mood, and busy working, too." You see, Lenny is a professional comedian and a

Gestalt therapist: a rather rare combination of careers. Yet in both, he teaches people to laugh instead of getting upset. He sees the humor in everything and humor certainly does keep him busy. Lenny presents his Laughter is the Best Therapy Workshop all over the world. I can vouch for the healing power of this non-serious therapeutic approach. Recently here in New Orleans, I watched as several of my clients made a dramatic shift in their coping mechanisms by practicing laughter as a first response to their troubles, instead of embracing their usual, familiar sadness, fear, anger, or guilt. The saying, "Fifty years from now, this'll be funny," didn't apply. It was funny right then and there.

I, too, am a Gestalt therapist. I was trained to help clients overcome depression and anxiety by having them express their long repressed negative feelings in my office. But for a while now, I have known that the real problem for most unhappy people is that their positive emotions are even more repressed than their negative ones. My first Gestalt teacher, Leland Johnson, believed that expressing all your feelings improved mental health. He had this little ditty he would say: "If you're sad, cry. If you're angry, shout. If you're afraid, shiver. If you're happy, laugh. If you're turned on, come!" Lenny's advice would be to laugh—along with all of the above. Lenny gives people permission to let their repressed love, joy, and humor up and out by encouraging them to laugh at anything, dance their troubles away, and never leave without a hug. He calls it a spiritual approach to happiness.

Preposterous? Yes. Effective? Very. I watched as he retrained the participants in his workshop to practice laughing to interrupt their usual stress reaction, whatever it usually was. Laughing immediately actually detoured them (and the people around them, too) from having those old familiar bad feelings. For the first time ever in their lives, several participants experienced the power of choosing a positive emotional reaction instead of the negative one they had learned in their family of origin in childhood. Many brought the exercise home to their partners that evening and for the first time in a long time, they laughed together, too.

Lenny's workshop has confirmed my long held belief that taking things too seriously is often the cause of depression in itself. Richard Bandler told me something very profound one evening years ago when I asked if a certain two people we knew were having a serious relationship. "I hope not," he wisecracked, "I hope they're having a fun one." I never forgot those words of wisdom or those of my guru, Jai, who gave me his Zen and the Art of Anxiety Reduction approach to mental health in just a few words: "Just tighten the loose ends and loosen the tight ends." Lenny's book specializes in loosening the tight ends.

Dorothy Parker, one of my favorite writers, penned a short poem describing herself at loose ends something like this: "The river's damp, the razor's sharp, I might as well live." Lenny would change that advice to "I might as well laugh." In his book, Lenny shares some of the depressing situations he has defused or redirected with humor. Considering some of the other far less effective emotional responses people have used to cope with their life difficulties, I applaud him for being a pioneer in not making seriousness even more serious. It takes courage to laugh, especially at yourself, and even more skill to get others to laugh with you at themselves. The rule of 'Laugh and the world laughs with you!' applies more often than not with Lenny. I hope the trend catches on worldwide. We might get The Hundredth Monkey laughing while he washes his sweet potatoes.

Lenny is my good friend and has been for over twenty years now. I am happy to publish his collection of funny stories. My only regret, however, is that his book is not yet a video tape. Then you would get to laugh at his live performance as I have. In fact, I'll start on that video project when I finish laughing at my regret. Or better yet, while I'm still laughing.

Anne Teachworth, Publisher
Gestalt Institute Press
Metairie/New Orleans, Louisiana

INTRODUCTION

This book was originally written in Hebrew, *Endless Optimism*. To date, it has sold over 50,000 copies, which is a major best seller in Israel. It was the winner of *The Israeli Book Award's Platinum Plaque*, July 1, 2001.

There is an optimistic story behind this book's history. I asked my Israeli publisher, Motti Panchevsky, how many copies I would have to sell in order to be considered a success in Israel.

"If you sell 10,000 copies, you are doing fine in Israel," he said.

"And if I sell 50,000 copies?" I asked.

"I'm in Seventh Heaven," he answered, as I detected a smile.

I was silent at first, and then I blurted, "I'll commit to selling 100,000 copies!" He had no response. And, of course, sales have not stopped.

I had to make that commitment in order to prove to him and to myself that it is not enough to write about laughter and optimism. We have to live it. Visualizing the good things in life, and making sure that they come true, is not just an illusion. It's a reality. We are all responsible for making our dreams become realities. It is therefore only natural that I predict that the English version of the book, *A Funny Thing Happened on the Way to Enlightenment* will become a global best seller. And it is only natural that my optimistic prediction should come true. Of course, dear reader, I'm going to need your help.

To those who have already helped me, I owe a certain amount of gratitude and appreciation. First off are my wife, Alisa, and my children, Natti, Dorone, and Ori, who, as usual, showered me with love and encouragement as they saw me through to the completion of both the Hebrew and English versions of a book that burned within me to be released.

Next is my publisher, Motti Panchevsky, of the Oranite Publishing Company in Israel, who suggested that I had a book to write after hearing me in a radio interview, thereby sparking the flame of passion that brought this book to light.

Lastly are those very special people who are, as friends, first among equals: my colleagues and friends, Dina Or, Miriam Bernhardt, and Rachael Ash, for their support all along our humorous journey; my sister Lorraine, who saw this manuscript and confirmed it even in its raw stage. And then there are my US publisher, Anne Teachworth, founding director of the Gestalt Institute of New Orleans, whom I love dearly, and Mackie Blanton, my editor for the Gestalt Institute Press, whom I also love dearly.

Finally, this note: Milton Berle (1909—2002) once observed, "*I do not steal jokes. I find them before they are lost.*" In Milton's spirit, I now would like to acknowledge all the sources of jokes, parables, and narratives that I've used to live my life laughing, sources visible and invisible, remembered and forgotten, cited and uncited, found and forever lost.

Lenny Ravich

CHAPTER ONE

Playing with Pain

The optimist sees the bagel while the pessimist concentrates on the hole.

—Anonymous

Humor and optimism as a way of life are a spiritual journey. All you need are three things to get on board:

One: To have won the *Great Sperm Race*
Two: To have been born at a very early age
Three: To have read this book

The first two you've already done successfully. Congratulations! Want proof? Isn't it true that billions of sperms were in that cruel race together with you? Billions of your brothers and sisters died along the way, because nature knows how to make sure that only the most beautiful, the fastest, and the strongest get to play this thing we call *Life*. Only one sperm out of billions made it to that once-a-month egg—and that's *YOU*. So the next time you're feeling a bit low, go to the mirror and whisper softly to that gorgeous creature staring back at you, "Baby, without you I'm nothing. You won the great sperm race! I'm me instead of somebody else!"

Wouldn't life be a bit more fun if instead of following

Shakespeare's observation that "all the world's a stage," we stepped off that stage now and then, ordered a quenching orange soda and some popcorn, took a seat in the audience, and watched our silly little drama called "life" from an aesthetic distance? But no more than three rows back and in the center, if you please. Taking life too seriously can be dangerous to one's health.

Living life as play could be a lot more powerful. You may get sick, but you'll have fun doing it. Seeing the absurdity in certain situations can make our journey a bit more tolerable. "You can dance life or you can drag it." *Be Here Now's* author, Ram Dass, exclaims. Or as my father used to say when I was suffering Shakespeare's "slings and arrows of outrageous fortune": "Some day you'll laugh at all this." Today I ask, "Why wait?"

We will never know how many people have been cured of a major illness or a minor depression through laughter. If prescriptions for laughter could be written and filled, there would undoubtedly be a sharp rise in the health and well-being of the population.

The paradox is that I spent most of my life paying a price for being funny and humorous. No one can claim to be a tutor in humor until he/she has experienced the tragic-comic paradoxes in his/her own life.

When I was in the seventh grade, I was placed in a special education class because I was diagnosed as being disturbed. In my mind, I labeled it "the dummy class." Now, as an adult, I'm still disturbed. However, I no longer get punished for it as I did in my childhood. Instead, I am rewarded with accolades, admiration, and money, because I write and lecture about the world as the disturbed, absurd, tragic comedy that it is.

Back to the "dummy" class. They (the supposedly know-it-all school officials) considered me disturbed because I didn't concentrate. And, quite frankly, why should I have? What I was taught I considered very boring. It was a hell of a lot more fun making the rest of the "dummies" in the class laugh at my antics. I used to mime eating peanut butter and jelly on crackers and it broke the kids up.

Their laughter was music to my ears. It made me think, "Wow, this is why I came into this world!" But there was a particular woman in class who couldn't tolerate my getting more attention than she did—the teacher. She just didn't know how to handle me. She'd been trained to teach her subject, not to deal with children. Looking back, it is easy to understand her. She was a teacher and had an obligation to complete the material before the end of the year. The pupils simply interfered with her noble goal.

The teacher sent me to the guidance counselor with the hope that she would solve "the problem"—me. Guidance counselors, by the way, are people who used to be teachers and then decided not to work any more. She would always call me "God" whenever she saw me. She would say, in desperation, "God, it's you again!" One day I arrived late to our session and she exclaimed, "Jesus Christ!" I declared, rather meekly, "I'm not Jesus Christ. I'm his father." In the USA, you're allowed to call someone else God, but if you declare that you are He, you get sent to a social worker.

The guidance counselor referred me to a social worker that couldn't stop smiling and asking questions.

"Leonard, does your mother tell you stories?" she inquired.

"Yes," I replied shyly.

"What kind of stories does she tell you?"

"How she was raped by the Cossacks," I answered sincerely.

The social worker referred me to a psychologist who came to my school to test my I.Q. level. He asked me to shake my head from side to side so that he could hear my "lonely" IQ bouncing around inside of my head. When I did, he claimed that he had heard it. I naively asked him to shake his head around. When he did, I blankly replied, "I don't hear anything at all in your head."

The principal's office at school was considered "holy ground" because it was where teachers lined up every week to collect their paychecks. One day, I passed by as they were queuing up. Amongst the group were the homeroom teacher, the guidance counselor, the social worker, and the school psychologist. I said to myself, "Hey, I'm financially supporting an entire team!"

I used to pray daily, "Dear God, please make me normal. Why did you have to create me funny? Why couldn't you make me like the other kids who come to school to take tests suffering from headaches, nausea and diarrhea?" The school I had attended had given me the feeling that I was not quite right. My mother saw me in my awesome mood and said something that impacted me for rest of my life. She said, "Lenny,"—(she used to call me Lenny because that's my name)—"I deserve the certificate from your school more than you do."

"Why?" I asked.

"Because I'm there more than you," she smiled.

It was then that I witnessed the wisdom of this approach of hers to life. She taught me to laugh at my problems. She took the lemons that life once in a while hands to all of us, put sugar on it, which is humor, and made lemonade. She made me laugh, and, with this, gain control of the situation. It's the same problem; only it looks a lot lighter. A great lesson was learned: Never take yourself too seriously. Remember, from lemons make lemonade.

I was referred to a psychiatrist, who, with all his certificates and diplomas, couldn't reach me. He only knew how to do one thing: give me pills.

"Here, take these pills before going to school," he declared solemnly.

"Why?" I asked him, and he explained that if I did as he ordered, I would feel better.

"I feel fine," I answered. "And not only that, but I think I'm too happy for my teachers as it is."

I took the pills every morning, and after two days there was no noticeable change. Everything was exactly the same . . . *only slower*. By the time I finally finished asking someone a question, they were already up the hallway in the toilet. I realized that I had no energy to eat my make-believe peanut butter and cracker sandwiches anymore. The only thing I could do was focus on my shoe. I stared at my shoe for hours at a time. They even had my father come to school so that he, too, could witness the improvement. If you don't think staring at your shoe is an educational advancement, I want to tell you that I received the best grades in my school career as long as I agreed to stay drugged.

Research emanating from the University of Chicago has suggested that children up to the age of six laugh as much as three hundred times a day. At the age of seven, their amount of laughter goes down to fifteen times a day. Do you know why? They went to school and got punished!

Many years later I became Supervisor of English for the Board of Education in Israel, and was subjected to witnessing children being punished in school by having to stand facing the wall. When I inquired as to what crime they had committed, the teacher explained, "They laughed during the lesson for no reason." Wonderful! Children are still being punished for being joyful. Why not put them on a rack and stretch them?

By the way, there is an upside to being in a special education class. The girls are fourteen and fifteen years old, and to a twelve-year-old boy, that's a real woman! To have come from the sixth grade with classmates who are flat-chested little girls, and find yourself sitting next to women who already wear lipstick and don sweaters to showcase the promised land right before your eyes, is a treat not to be taken lightly. There was one particular young girl in my class who had incredible buttocks. I used to ask the teacher if she would invite Doris to the blackboard to work out math problems so I could enjoy this miraculous view.

You are perhaps wondering how a child from a special education class in the States gets to be a supervisor of English teachers in Israel? But, you see, this just goes to show you what a sorry state the Israeli Educational System is in.

The ability to play with pain, as I had learned from my mother, was rediscovered when I began to read Shalom Aleichem, Isaac Bashevis Singer, and Woody Allen. I would get to the end of their stories and was struck with the dilemma of not knowing whether to laugh or to cry. I realized that this ability to play with pain was the Jew's style of survival. I witnessed this in a film I once viewed where a gang of gentiles chased a Jewish youth and beat him mercilessly, breaking his glasses in the process. This scenario went on for some time until, one day, the Jew saw the Gentiles coming to beat him up again; so he removed his glasses, threw them on the floor, and smashed them under foot at his own will. "I'll do it to myself before they do it to me!" This is the Jew's way of playing with pain. Whenever I appear in front of audiences, large or small, I begin my presentation by saying, "You all don't know this, but in a little while you are going to give me a standing ovation." I ask them to please stand up, and they give me exactly what I asked for.

I also follow the formula of *SW-SW-SW* that I learned from Jack Canfield, co-author of the *Chicken Soup For The Soul* series of texts. I gather the courage to ask for what I want and the possibility is that of *SW*—Some will give it to me, that is. The other possibility is also *SW*—Some won't give it to me. And the other *SW* is *So what?!*

Optimists won't ever give up on their dreams, because they believe that there is another SW out there—"Someone's Waiting." I find that when I get the embarrassment and insecurity of "Will I be good enough?" out of the way, and poke a little fun at myself, my Someone's Waiting bonds the audience to me and me to them quickly and humorously.

Walter E. O'Connell (1990) discovered that the humorist is the person with self-training in the growth of self-esteem. One of my Someones once told me, "Don't take life too seriously. You won't get out of it alive anyway."

CHAPTER TWO

Bullfighting through Life

Life is suffering, misery and pain, and it's over too quickly.
—Woody Allen

I follow a formula that I learned from Jack Canfield, co-author of the series entitled Chicken Soup for the Soul. The formula is $E + R = O$. **E** is the event, or whatever happens to us in life. **R** is our response to what happens to us. We sometimes have no control over what happens to us, but we do have the power to choose our response to what happens to us. And **O** is the outcome, how we feel, how we behave, how we think, as a result of the response we choose to what happens to us. Martin E.P. Seligman, PhD., in his book *Learned Optimism* (1990), states that one of the most significant findings in psychology in the last twenty years is that individuals can choose the way they think.

This could be explained more clearly if we try to imagine life as a bullfight. In a bullfight there is the toreador who holds a red cape to the side of him as he baits the bull. The bull, with all its power and strength, charges the cape, not harming the toreador, because, of course, the toreador is wise enough to hold the cape away from his body. The bull, to me, signifies life, with all its confrontations and exacerbations. The red cape is the metaphor I use for the ego. I believe that putting the ego to the side will cause a lot less mental anguish. I once heard someone say: "Pain is inevitable. Suffering is an option."

Most people I know live life as a bullfight, but instead of holding the cape to the side, they start each day by holding the cape directly in front of them. The outcome is clear. BOOM! The bull comes smashing into the cape, and takes the person holding the cape into a reality of pain. Then we say, "That person takes things to heart." Some people hold the cape near the stomach area and we say, "That person is eaten up with worry." Or: "It hit me right in the gut." The hospitals are full of people who take things to heart and consume themselves up in pain and worry. What we are dealing with here is stress-related illnesses. That's because life to them is like going bowling. They throw the ball down the alley, and when it doesn't go exactly where they want it to, they make faces, thinking that maybe crouching down in a pained expression might have an influence on the ball. Like the ball really cares! Sheesh!!

As Wayne Dyer, author of *Pull Your Own Strings*, has stated: "I used to get upset when caught in traffic jams, until I realized that the traffic jams don't really care."

Let me give you some examples of how the world, in using the formula of $E+R=O$, would look with the cape held to the side.

Drivers and their passengers alike are aware of the tension and aggression that greet us the moment we engage other drivers. Have you observed that some traffic lights are audio-visual? At the speed of light, red changes to green and—*beep-beep!* The driver in the car in back of us, who lacks patience, wants to have patience and he wants it now! At the screeching of brakes, which is enough to cause spasms, you might find the other driver communicating in sign language something to the effect that you're nuts, by holding his finger to his head, meaning, "You need a shrink!"

If my cape is too close to my body, the bull smashes in and I become irritated, and, as a result, I cause my entire day to be spoiled by anger. In addition, I self-poison my body with a rapid increase in my blood pressure. If I take a breath, and put the cape to the side, I may choose to see a poor fellow suffering from a headache. Why else would he be pointing to his head if this weren't so? I communicate to him in sign language, as I raise my open hands as if to declare, "I'm sorry, I have no aspirin."

I have used the $E+R=O$ formula many times. I remember when I took my youngest son to be registered in the first grade at school. A female doctor interviewed him. At one point she turned to me, and without warning, asked me if he masturbates. My spontaneous reply was, "Not any more than his father does."

The principal of the same school invited me to a meeting in which he told me, "As a result of your son's behavior, he ought to be placed in an institution." I agreed, but told him that in order to do that, he would have to get the signature of the municipal social worker. He asked me if I knew her name. I paused and said, "Yes, she's my wife, and she's also an excellent social worker."

What's life without humor and a good laugh? A day that goes by without a belly laugh at absurd situations or at ourselves is a real pity. Mahatma Gandhi once observed, "Without a sense of humor, I would have committed suicide long ago." So they killed him.

Viktor E. Frankl, a Holocaust victim and author of *Man's Search for* Meaning, wrote that the Nazis had the power to take away everything in life from him except one thing: his freedom to respond to what had happened to him in any way that he chose. If he chose to see the death camp as an opportunity rather than as a tragedy, he would grow and become stronger as a result of it, rather than becoming a victim and succumb. He chose life, and lived to tell about it. If we look at Life and ourselves in this light, then everything that happens to us, good or bad, is an opportunity to learn and grow. Frankl regarded the sense of humor as part of a person's capacity for self-detachment.

I shared this wisdom with a doctor who was studying with me at my Gestalt Institute. "Anthony," I told him," if you change the word *problem* to *opportunity,* things will appear much lighter. There are no problems in life, only opportunities." At that moment he received a call on his beeper. "I've got to go," he exclaimed, "there are suddenly a lot of opportunities piling up in the emergency room."

The Academy Award winning foreign film Life Is Beautiful tells the story of how a father protects his son while imprisoned in a Nazi camp by projecting the event as a game. He explains that the game is based on points, and whoever works the hardest and fastest gets the most points, and the winner is awarded with a tank. Of course, the child believes his father, and at the film's end, the child is driven away in a tank. You get exactly what you believe you deserve is the message I came away with. I also witnessed the formula $E+R=O$ in its most creative process as a result of having seen this movie.

When my eldest son was fourteen (and too young to get a driver's license), he stole my car. When I found out about it, I wasn't the least bit surprised, because when I was his age, I had done exactly the same thing with my father's car. The car that my son had stolen was called a *Sussita*—an automobile known only in Israel and long considered by Israelis as the car you'd be most likely to find at the top of the heap, and in large numbers at that, at the junkyard. It was such a rotten model of Israeli technology that this vehicle was banished forever from being produced again.

I once parked my *Sussita* in Tel-Aviv and made sure the lock on the driver's wheel was secure. When I got back, I noticed someone had stolen the lock from my car, instead of stealing the whole bloody vehicle. The car wasn't even good enough for a common thief!

Anyway, as my son was hot-rodding his way through town, the police tried to flag him down without success. Finally, they simply cut in front of him, causing him to come to a screaming halt. He was promptly arrested and hauled off to jail. When my wife and I were informed of his arrest, we rushed to the police station. Upon seeing my son's painful face, I said to him, "I'm disappointed in you. Couldn't you steal a BMW? At least you could have given them a good car chase in a more elegant manner!" He laughed heartily and the tension between us was released.

The formula $E+R=O$ once came in handy while trying to get some information from my bank clerk. Each time he began to explain something, the phone rang and he would discontinue his conversation with me in order to take the call. After repeating this act a few more times, I calmly took out my cellular phone and asked him for his telephone number. He asked me why I would want to talk to him on his cell phone when I was already talking to him in person. I told him that I had noticed that the phone was receiving priority and that I preferred to talk with him without interruption. We both smiled as he got the message in a more humorous manner.

I love the story of the overly sensitive insurance salesman who, when trying to sell a policy to a potential customer, would take the customer's "no" as personal rejection. He soon noticed, however, that for every nine people who refused his policy, the tenth was bound to accept. He therefore observed that the tenth person bought a policy that made him $2,500 richer. So he put the cape to the side, chose a different response that would allow each person who refused him to receive a "thank you" from him for the $250. He decided that he was going to get $2,500 at the end of being refused, so why not thank the nine people who contributed to the kitty? Even if their answer was going to be "no," it was better than feeling rejected.

As Martin E.P. Seligman has noted: "Optimistic individuals produce more than pessimists do. The optimist bounces back from defeat, picks up and starts again."

When my three children were growing up, I made sure that they became my captive audience. I entertained them at every possible occasion and most enjoyed their giggles and applause. I was their comic and guru of entertainment. I loved it! But something happened over the years. I suddenly found that the tables had been turned. Now, at festivities, meals, and evenings together, I had suddenly been reluctantly forced into becoming their audience. Such a reversal of roles is difficult and uncomfortable, to say the least. Whenever I nowadays try to get a joke in, or start declaiming like a wise old soothsayer, they quickly jump in with a look of disgust, adding, "Dad, puhleese! You're just not funny!" This is followed by their imitation of an airplane nose-diving, crashing, and burning in its destruction with a loud, "*Yeerrrougghh . . . crrruussh!!!*" In front of other people, this is most humiliating!

I must warn of pitfalls in using humor with super-serious people who find it difficult to play around. While I was a high school teacher, I always felt that teaching and learning must be an experience much like an evening at the theater. There must be laughter, love or tears; because without these elements, there was no sense in teaching or learning.

One day, while I was taking a break between the classes that I was teaching, the principal requested that I come to see him. He showed me a letter written by my tenth grade class committee. I was shocked. They wanted me replaced by another teacher. They claimed, "It is impossible trying to learn anything with this clown. All he does is make us laugh." I gave them each an A. Their grammar and spelling were perfect!

CHAPTER THREE

Playing with the Absurd

Don't grow up. See the world through a child's eyes.
—Bernard Segal

I can't help comparing people, countries, mentalities and cultures. When I moved to Israel from the USA, I was constantly being asked my opinion of Israeli culture. After pondering Mahatma Gandhi's response, my reply was, "Yes, that could be a great idea."

In Israel when someone tells you to be at a certain place at a certain time, he means a half-hour to an hour later. And even that's not too sure. When I traveled to London, I noticed the difference. I bought a ticket for a play that was to begin at 8:00 P.M. I'm so used to "Israeli Very Mean Time" rather than "Greenwich Mean Time" that I arrived a bit late. The usher would not allow me to enter the theater. I inquired as to why I wasn't allowed to go in. He looked me straight in the eye, and said with his brisk British accent, "This is not Tel-Aviv, Sir." I wondered how he had known where I was from, since I speak English with an American accent. I was then asked to proceed to the waiting room to be called for the second act. When I got there, I understood right away how he knew where I was from. The waiting room was completely full. Nobody spoke English—only Hebrew.

Selling your car in Israel forces you to become a marketing expert. Trade-ins with car dealers are so humiliating that you have to put your own ads in the newspaper, take phone calls and handle negotiations as if you owned a dealership. This way, at least, you have a choice by whom to be humiliated. Then, when a potential buyer examines your car, you are lowered to worm level by their growling under the hood, finding a scratch here and a dent there; all this energy invested with the hope of bringing down the price. When I finally succeeded in selling my car, I asked the buyer if he was happy with the price. He said he wasn't. He asked me if I was happy with the deal. I said I wasn't. That satisfied both of us! Selling a car in Israel means both buyer and seller must be miserable. That makes us both joyous!

Funny things happen to all of us, although we may not view them as being humorous as they are happening. The difference is that I see the humor in the absurdity of differences, and anybody who wants to can do the same.

An example of this was my choice to live in a development town called Nazareth Elite, Israel. Everyone I met was truly surprised that I, a born and bred American, would actually want to live in a development town, when I could easily choose to live in the "big city," Tel-Aviv.

My response is: It's all in how you look at it. In America, I had met many people who worked in New York, for example, and lived in New Jersey or the Connecticut suburbs. Now, that's about an hour and a half traveling time. When I asked them why they would prefer to travel so long a distance, when they could very well live much closer to work, they each replied something like this: "In the cities there's crime, violence, homelessness, noise, and pollution. It's worth the longer trip to and from work, because in the suburbs I have a much larger home with a view and clean air, even if the house did cost me three times as much." Quality of life, they called it. That sounded good to me.

Upon arriving in Israel, I noticed that everything was the opposite. People paid a fortune to be right smack in the middle of crime, pollution, noise, violence, and the homeless. Because my wife is a Zabarit (a native born Israeli. Nobody's perfect!), she insisted on living in the center of this turmoil.

So we went to Tel-Aviv to buy a condo. While shopping around, and finally arriving at these so-called living quarters, I noticed, upon entering the apartment, that I could hear, for the first time in my life, the neighbor's toilet flushing. And if that wasn't enough, when I opened the window, I could see him flushing it as clear as day. I asked the real estate agent what the price of this abode was (only available in the middle of Dante's "Inferno") and was told that I'd have to cough up $100,000. This was in 1973. Today, this same piece of dreck costs $300,000. I told my wife that this was ridiculous, and that I was going to try to find something more livable in the suburbs of Tel-Aviv. A suburb to an American is about an hour and a half outside the maddening city; so I traveled north for about an hour and a half.

I finally arrived at this model of an American suburb. What a view! Americans would pay tons for this panorama engulfing the Jezereel Valley, Mount Tabor, The Churchill Forests (Hey, Beverly Hills!). I stopped a teen-ager and asked him the name of this Tel-Aviv suburb.

"Nazareth Elite," he responded.

"Where can I inquire about prices and availability?" I asked.

He pointed to the direction of a small hut.

I walked in and was immediately greeted by a salesman who offered me his smile and a strong cup of Turkish coffee. I began to feel around for prices, knowing full well that I could never afford a home in the suburbs of Tel-Aviv. I figured that if that stinking apartment in the middle of the cauldron known as Tel-Aviv cost $100,000, then surely, this villa I was talking about with the great view had to be in the vicinity of at least $250,000 to $300,000.

The salesman took out a sheet of paper, looked at it, took a sip of his Turkish coffee and then calmly said, "Mr. Ravich, that villa you had in mind is ready for sale."

He took another sip of coffee and then continued.

"You can have it for IL80,000 Lira."

I was stunned! I couldn't believe what I'd just heard!! This couldn't be! IL80,000 Lira in 1973 was equivalent to $18,000. A villa in the Tel-Aviv suburbs, with an astounding view for $18,000? This joker's got to be kidding, I thought to myself.

So I said, "Listen, joker, you've got to be kidding!"

Little did I know that in Israel when you're negotiating purchases, and you say, "You've got to be kidding"—they lower the price!

Out of my innocence I had become a hard-nosed, negotiating businessman.

"Mr. Ravich! Sit down, please," he offered, pointing to a chair. "We can make a deal. How about a IL20, 000 Lira down payment, and the rest, the IL50,000, you pay off every month as mortgage?"

Wait a minute! I'm going to get this gorgeous cottage in the Tel-Aviv Mountains for a down payment of a mere $6,000?! He's got to be pulling my leg!

So I said, "You're pulling my leg."

Here we go again. He stood up and said, "I can make it easier for you. What about your Standing Loan?"

"What's a Standing Loan?" I gasped.

"The government gives you a loan and you don't pay it back. That is, if you promise to live in that house for five years, and you keep your promise, you owe nothing on the loan," he explained.

"What a great country!" I blurted out.

People told me it would be difficult living in Israel and not to move there. But this is heaven. I hadn't been clued in yet that this Standing Loan was a sweetener made to lure people away from that junk heap, Tel-Aviv, to live in a development town, which is positively slumming for a city slicker. I was born in the USA, and to me it was a suburb, so what the hell! I put the down payment on the house and walked merrily once a month to the post office to pay my mortgage. (In Israel, mortgage payments are made at the post office.)

One day thereafter, I was standing in line to pay my mortgage. I noticed something very peculiar. I looked at the stamp on the envelope, which was sent to me in order to pay my mortgage. I realized, at that moment, that the stamp on the envelope was worth more than the mortgage. I asked a young man standing next to me in line, "What country in the world would send you a notification to pay your mortgage with a stamp that costs more than the payment?" Without looking up from his newspaper, he said, "Inflation." I was later to learn that the Israeli Lira was not tied to an index and that during the horrible inflation in Israel during the 1970s, prices were soaring, but the mortgages remained fixed. I'm not a genius when it comes to the subject of economy, so I was extremely confused.

Upon arriving to my home, I spotted a man in my garden looking around as if he were searching for something. So I approached him and inquired if I could be of some help. He asked me if I knew Lenny Ravich.

"I hope so, because I'm Lenny Ravich," I responded.

My answer drew a stunned look from the gentleman.

"What! You're a man?"

I had recently just learned that the name Lenny, in Israel, is a woman's name. It's short for Elana.

I have never being one to resist a little playfulness.

"Well, to tell you the truth, so many interesting things have been happening to me lately, that I'm not quite sure. But I'll check it for you," I answered.

I checked, and to my great fortune, it was still there.

"Yes, I'm still a member of the male species," I said after having examined myself. "How can I be of service to you?"

"You must give me all the money for this house now! I'm from the mortgage office," he groused at me brusquely, looking me straight in the eye.

"But I pay my mortgage every month at the post office," I pleaded.

He finally gave me a smile and asked, "You don't understand Hebrew well, do you?"

Now that he had me transfixed with that little bit of tweaking, he continued on: "You see, the government has depleted all the zeroes from the Lira. This happened on Monday. We are now using a new currency called the Israeli Shekel."

I immediately began to feel the perspiration under my arms,

seeping through my shirt and nervously asked, "What's a Shekel? How much do I owe you?"

"Seven Shekels," was his sincere reply.

I couldn't wait any longer. I began writing to all my friends and family in the States, and around the world to come as quickly as possible to live in Israel. I explained that they could buy a gigantic house in the mountains of Tel-Aviv with an incredible view for as little as seven shekels! And don't forget the Standing Loan!

So where is heaven and where is hell? Some wise ones among us know exactly where they are. Both are in our mind, and we choose which one we want from moment to moment. Some might think I'm living in hell because I reside in a development town. Others might agree with me that I'm in heaven because I live in the suburbs.

In *Pirkei Avot (The Sayings of the Fathers)*, a question is asked and answered: *Who is rich? The one who chooses to be happy with what he has.*

After having lived in Nazareth Elite for twenty-seven years, I decided to change addresses and move to Tel-Aviv. Some people reacted immediately.

"My goodness, you are in the heart of Tel-Aviv!" they exclaimed.

"You got it all wrong. I'm in the asshole of Tel-Aviv!" I would retort.

I've noticed the absurdity of differences and I've learned to see the humor in it. For example, as an American, born and educated, I register for conferences, take trips, or plan lessons months in advance. I remember registering for a Humor Conference in Saratoga Springs, New York. The forms were filled out, airline tickets purchased, and even taxis were put on alert at least two months before the event.

My friend, Gingy Goldberg, a well-known comic in Israel, made it quite certain that he, too, wanted to attend this same conference. We sat down a few times together to scan the pre-conference program for the very best lectures available at this workshop. I, of course, sent in all of my registration material before the announced deadline, not resting until everything was 100% okay. Whenever I asked Gingy if he had registered or booked his flight, his typical Israeli response was, "It'll be all right." He never even bothered to sign up for the conference. This is typical Israeli behavior. The cosmos was created as their playpen. No need to think ahead!

I left for the States without him, and while in the lobby of the hotel where the conference was to take place, whom do I see? Gingy!

"How did you get here?" I exclaimed.

"By bus," he answered matter-of-factly.

"Have you signed up?" I asked.

"No, not yet," he replied casually.

"But when will you register?" I almost shouted.

"Lenny, *It'll be all right*," he calmly emphasized.

"Where are you going to sleep?" I insisted, pressing on.

"In your room," he smiled.

He not only slept in my room, and got a 15% discount at the conference center, but he also left me with a $30 phone bill, as well. I had to laugh. What was the choice?

And what about the differences on the airlines? Only on El-Al Airline do you hear the captain blurt over the loud speaker, "Sit down, for God's sake!" Now I know what "stand-by" means on El-Al. The minute the belt sign goes off, everyone starts "standing by." Israelis get up and walk around and talk to everyone as if they were their cousins; and the plane hasn't even left Tel-Aviv yet. I think it has something to do with the "wandering Jew" syndrome. For two thousand years we've been wandering around from place to place and today we can't control that urge, even on a flight.

I always wondered why on El Al flights the wing tips to the left, comes back up, and flaps down again. I looked to the back of the plane and understood why. A group of religious Jews davening (saying the evening prayers with their traditional forward and backward rocking movements) causes this phenomenon.

Little kids on these flights are not disciplined either. Their parents allow them to run up and down the aisle, laughing, crying, and screaming. On one flight, this boy of about eight years old, who was sitting in the seat directly in back of me, wouldn't stop kicking my chair. I got up and walked over to him.

"How would you like to play outside?" I asked, bending down directly over him, smiling, of course. I learned that response in a lecture given by Sam Horn, author of the book, *Conzentration*. I have always admired the ability to capture an emotion or a situation in a quick, pithy image.

For example, I once asked an Israeli stewardess why the flight was so bumpy. She replied, "We have a new pilot on this flight and he finds it difficult taking his foot completely off the brakes."

Some images, on the other hand, are laden with unintentional irony. When the captain of a flight makes the announcement, "We are flying at the height of 30,000 feet," I muse to myself, "Oh, I'm so happy for that piece of information! Now, if the plane goes into a nose dive, I'll know exactly how much time I have to pray."

Have you ever noticed that on major international airlines there is a sign on the chair in front of you admonishing, "Please fasten seat belts while seated"? Do they really expect me to mistakenly fasten the seat belt while I'm standing?

When Israelis meet each other abroad, without even having to know each other, their first questions are centered around the price of things, and about who paid less for what. The game is: Don't be the first to answer. No matter what you have paid for something, the ante is sure to be lowered by the second player. Then you will have to live with the embarrassment of being labeled a sucker.

Israeli men have a problem with asking directions. It isn't macho; they have to guess. Even if his girl or wife begs him to ask directions, he figures, (according to the comedian, Yakov Smirnov) that the world is round and if he continues in the same direction, eventually he will end up in the same place. Besides, they're making good time moving fast.

I really think it's an inter-generational thing handed down to us by Moses. I mean, here he was wandering around the desert for forty years, and all he had to do was ask directions. It goes back even further. Think of all those billions of sperm trying to get to that one egg. All they have to do is ask!

Most Israeli men lack any appreciation for the finer things in a home. If you advise an Israeli bachelor where he could hang some pictures, his inevitable answer will be, "What pictures? The wall is fine the way it is. Good enough!"

Some owners of restaurants have a fly painted in the urinals in the men's room. They are aware that while an Israeli man is urinating, he will inevitably mistake the painted fly for a real one. He will invariably attempt to "piss it off." By the time he finds out that the fly is nothing but an artistic expression, the game is over. It's too late. He keeps aiming at the dummy fly. The toilet floor in these restaurants are therefore always dry. No Israeli man ever misses the urinal! Hats off to these creative café owners.

Something happened to me as an English teacher in high school in Israel that would probably never happen anywhere else. On one particular day, I felt a bit feverish and told the secretary of the school that I had a sore throat and decided to go home. I couldn't believe my ears when she demanded that I open my mouth so that she could examine my throat. Hesitating, I then inquired, "I also have hemorrhoids. Would you like to examine them, too?"

Only in Israel: I bought a fish at the supermarket only to get home and find that it was rotten. I brought it back to the manager and told him that I wanted another fish in place of the one I had bought.

"Why?" he inquired.

"Because it's rotten," I answered.

"Then, why did you buy it in the first place?" he, feigning puzzlement, responded cooly.

I think that the income tax people in Israel should shorten the process of filing tax forms every year. The form should have two simple blanks to fill in. One: How much did you earn last year? Two: Send it in!

God created the world in seven days. On the sixth day He/She created Israel. He/She told His/Her angels, "Look at this lovely pearl of a country I'm making for the Jews. It's tiny, but I've made sure that there will be snow-capped mountains in the north, fresh water in the center, miles of beaches, and a large desert in the south." The angels were astonished.

"All that for the Jews? Don't you think you're being too generous?"

"I don't think so," God answered, and then chuckled: "Wait till you see the neighbors I'm planning to give them."

I think that to search for answers and to always find them would make the game of life dull.

CHAPTER FOUR

Laughing with the Past

The world is wounded. Everyone is wounded.
                                    —Bernard Segal

It's quite difficult trying to lighten up, when we are carrying a lot of baggage from the past. One way to deal with some of the pain, anger, fears, and misfortunes of the past is to find the humor in things and then to laugh at them. Anyone who tells me they had an easy time growing up is heavy into forgetting. "It's never too late to have a happy childhood," Tim Robbins, author of *Still Life with Woodpecker*, has observed.

My childhood was confusing. On the one hand my family loved me beyond comprehension; on the other, I was the family punching bag. I was known as Samson in my neighborhood since I had hair all over my back. Whenever one of the members in my family decided to "educate" me, my back was the target for all of their unfinished business and past rages. I was their therapy punching and kicking sack. Nature creatively protects its species by covering places vulnerable to open wounds with lots of hair. Hence: much hair on my back and the nickname of Samson.

My task was to fulfill my sister's fantasies. When I was seven and she was fourteen, we went to see a film starring Tyrone Power. When we got home, she insisted that I kiss her like Tyrone Power had done in that last scene when he saved the girl. She was to be the girl.

"I can't reach you," I protested.

"Then stand on that chair and kiss me like Tyrone Power," she would insist.

I had to keep going back to see that movie until I got it right. It wasn't like today with video and stop motion, slow motion, fast forward, and rewind. I had to buy a ticket, see the film again, leave at the end and go back to the cashier's window to purchase another ticket in order to view that last scene again, and then back to the ticket window and on and on until I thought that I could get it right.

When I was nine, my sixteen-year-old sister announced that I was to learn to play the trumpet. She had thrown Tyrone Power over for her newfound love, Harry James, a famous bandleader and a very sweet-sounding trumpet player. I was much more interested in his wife, Betty Grable, who was the number one pin-up for the GIs during the Second World War. At my sister's persistent and bothersome urging, I begged my mother to buy me a trumpet.

"Why, who is she in love with now?" my mother slyly inquired.

I did learn to play trumpet. For music lessons, I turned to our local Italian barber, Johnny. For a dollar a lesson, Johnny taught me the musical scales and then some. My mother was quite satisfied because this solved the problem of my needing braces on my teeth, which were, and still are, rather protruding. She figured she would kill three birds with one stone: I would learn to become a trumpet player, my sister would get her fantasies fulfilled, and my buck teeth would eventually straighten out, if I would only just practice enough by pressing the mouthpiece to my lips. None of the above worked, however.

These fantasies of hers were tolerable, until the day that she let it be known that she was now in love with Willy Pep, the Featherweight Champion of the world. When I saw boxing gloves in my room, I knew the time had come to start taking boxing lessons. And you know what? I did. And to this day I'm a sucker for kissing, listening to trumpet concertos, watching boxing matches, and fantasizing my being in the ring with the best of them.

I know that it wasn't easy for any of us growing up. I think that with all the anger I once had for my parents and sister, they were doing the best they could do at that time. I don't believe that my parents got up every morning and said to one another, "How many ways can we think of to screw up our son today?" They did what they knew how. How many of us think that our parents didn't love us enough because we never got from them what we really wanted?

But, then again, how many of us actually asked for what we really wanted? We might have thought to ourselves, "If they really loved me, they should have known what I wanted without my asking them." Well, I don't know of too many parents who are professional mind readers. We wanted them to be that which was impossible, and when they didn't fulfill our expectations, we felt they didn't love us enough; or that we weren't deserving of whatever it was that we wanted.

To this day, some of us are still afraid to ask for what we want because deep down inside we feel that since our parents denied us, who would think us worthy enough to give us what we want? So we begin to concentrate on other people's needs rather than our own, believing that others' desires are more important than our own. Our parents only did what their parents did to them. We have the opportunity to undo the cycle.

Try humor.

I still carry my family around in my head. Whenever I go to a restaurant, I never order from the food side of the menu. I always order from the price list. If I see a salad I like, and another that happens to be a few cents cheaper, I order the cheaper one, even though I might dislike it intensely. But it's cheaper. I'm saving money, you see. When the salad I didn't want is finally served, I have to finish it all, because I will have to pay for it! If you asked me how I enjoyed my meal, my answer would have invariably been Woody Allen's, "The meal was terrible! And there wasn't enough!"

Whenever I go shopping and I stop to look at something I would like to buy, my mother's voice goes off in my head: "Tsi fiel. Daft nisht." In Yiddish, this means, "It costs too much. You don't need it."

It's okay for me to buy the most expensive goods for my children or my wife, but when it actually comes to paying for something for myself, I break out into a sweat. To this day, I get care packages from my sister, who sends me her children's "hand-me-ups." Otherwise, I would have nothing to wear.

The same is true for flying trans-Atlantic. My accountant has practically begged me to fly business class. He tells me it's a recognized expense and that I deserve it because I have a small business. Again, the sweat and the recorded message, "Tsi fiel." I can actually hear my mother shouting, at the top of her lungs, *"You can get to where you're going just as fast by flying Economy Class!"*

I don't allow myself to take a vacation. Seriously. I've tried several times, only to hear my mother's voice in her Yiddish accent going off in my head.

"So what's this loafing all about? What are you, some kind of a banker?"

The only way I allow myself some time off is if the vacation I'm taking involves some kind of study program along with it, or an invitation to facilitate a workshop. Only then will I take a day or two to kick back. It's as if I'm trying to appease that voice in my head by saying, "See, Mom, I had to fly to London, I'm studying there."

I especially identify with my friend Dina Or when she tells me," I'll never be a workaholic. A workaholic takes her work home. I'm never home!"

I think Freud was right when he said that we marry our parents. I once planned to surprise my wife on our wedding anniversary. I ordered tickets for a flight to Eilat (Israel's lush resort area on the Red Sea), where I had booked a suite for the weekend. I planned to tell her that I had to give a lecture in Tel-Aviv, invite her to come with me, and instead of going to the said address, drive her to the airport and sweep her off her feet.

I approached her while she was reading her newspaper.

"Come with me to my lecture," I whispered excitedly.

"I've heard you before," she said numbly, without looking up from the paper.

"But there are some interesting people there I want you to meet," I pleaded in total panic.

"I haven't got time for your so-called 'interesting people'," she grunted, turning the page.

"Okay!" I loudly declared. "You have succeeded in screwing up my surprise for our anniversary. I booked a flight and a hotel in Eilat. Come on, anyway."

"A flight!" she screamed, looking up from her paper for the first time. "You want to fly? What's wrong with the buses in this country? They're not good enough for you?"

Get my point? My mother, my wife!

I like to cook, but my wife interferes by telling me which pot or frying pan to use.

"Here, use this one without the handles," she insists, handing me a very old pot minus the handles. "You've already burnt all my good pots."

And when I come home, she asks, "Are you hungry?" When the answer is in the affirmative, she orders, "Change your clothes. I like that shirt you are wearing, and you always spill food all over yourself. And try not to drop food all over the floor!"

Did I marry my mother, or what?

My wife calls me on my cell phone. When I answer with," Yes, Hello?" She asks, "Lenny, is that you?" Who does she think it is? George?

Have you noticed that the telephone always rings at the wrong time? That the alarm clock always goes off at the wrong time? That your mate always wants to have that "serious talk" with you at the wrong time?

To this day, I still eat standing over the sink. My mother used to make me a sandwich, pull up a chair, and order, "Here, stand on this and eat over the sink."

The crumbs, you know.

My wife always asks me to eat the stale bread first, before eating the fresh bread. Brett Leake (a very funny sit-down comic) reminds me of the logic in this line of thinking. If you do this, you can eat the stale bread while the fresh bread gets stale. He also helps me to understand the hidden meaning of what my wife means when she insists, "If you don't finish the soup, I'll have to throw it out." That's also a great choice. It's either the garbage disposal or me!

I find looking back hilarious. I remember my mother eating garlic before she went to sleep every night. She explained that if the Angel of Death should dare to come into her room to take her while she was asleep, she had planned to wake up and ask, "Whooo is it?" The Angel of Death, getting a whiff of the garlic would have no choice but to declare, "Echh Pluch! I'll come back tomorrow!" And then The Angel of Death would just fly away. She was sure that this got her extra time on this planet.

My mother always laughed with all her heart. But underneath, there was always a strong indication of inner pain. At the end of her belly laughter, she would inevitably let out with a long sigh of "Oy!" When talking on the phone, I would hear her declaring, "Oy! Oy! Oy! That's terrible. So what's gonna be?"

"What are you talking about, Mom?" I would ask with much concern.

"The weather," she would declare.

If ever someone called up and exclaimed that every thing was fantastic, she would slam the phone down, exclaiming in turn, "Sorry, wrong number!"

Whenever I said something positive about myself or gave compliments to her, my mother was quick to spit twice over her shoulder, "Tfoo! Tfoo!" And we were never to mention any money that we might be happy to have received. That was good for a loud, "Sha!" from her. Her searching for some wood to knock on or some salt to throw over her shoulder followed this. This was because there was some kind of a legacy handed down that you had to be careful not to succeed too much, or, God forbid, talk about it, unless you were ready to face the inevitable catastrophe that was bound to fall upon you because of your good fortune. Some called it The Evil Eye.

I'm absolutely certain that all of this has to do with *The Book of*

Job from the Hebrew Bible. Job, one of the rich and healthy of his land, and also bestowed with much honor, loses it all as the Devil tests him with a wager about his loyalty to God. We had to be careful not to talk about how good we really felt. Better not to feel good at all. "Careful! If you laugh in the morning, you'll cry at night."

My mother used to tell me stories almost every day. One was about the Cossacks nearly raping her, and the other was one that binds Jewish boys and their Jewish mothers into a very unusual life-script. She used to tell me about a little boy who always told his mother how much he loved her.

Years later, when he became a young bachelor, he met a girl and proposed marriage. She said she would marry him only on one condition. He must take a knife, go home, cut his mother's heart out, and bring the heart to her. That way the girl would be sure that he truly loved her. So the young man bought a dagger, went home and cut his mother's heart out.

With his mother's still beating heart in hand, he hurried to his future bride. On the way, he stumbled and fell. It was then that he heard the heart murmur softly to him, "Be careful, my son. Don't hurt yourself. Are you all right?"

I later discovered that other Jewish mothers told their young Jewish sons the same story.

I came to the conclusion that with all the laughter and fun in my family, there was always an underlying message of doom. In my parents' house you were never allowed to feel healthily empowered with such *I love* sentences as "I love myself. I love money. I love success. I love winning. I love being famous. I love power. I love the adulation of others. I love sex."

Sex?! Are you kidding? Absolutely forbidden to mention the subject! My sister was told that she had to remain a virgin till she married. She was taught that sex was dirty, disgusting, and filthy, but that she was to *save it for the one she loved!*

The only time my father talked to me about sex was when he warned me not to masturbate. "Too late," was my immediate response. I was thirty-four at the time; so I really didn't know what this conversation was all about.

"Why not masturbate, Dad? Woody Allen says that masturbation is an opportunity to have sex with someone you really love," I quoted with much smugness.

"You'll get feeble-minded from it," he threatened.

"Can I do it until I start slurring my speech?" was my innocent indulgence.

Whenever I was in the company of people who had trouble remembering names, I would walk up to them and quietly whisper, "You, too?"

When I was a child, we were told that to have strong bones and teeth we should drink as much as six glasses of milk a day. Then, once the research was done on this notion, investigators found that milk is hazardous to one's health. Eggs, we were told, had vitamin D; so we were to eat eggs as much as possible. Later, however, we discovered that eggs could kill you. Salt tablets were distributed to workers who perspired. Later, we were told, salt will kill you.

And then meat will kill you. Don't eat hamburgers. They will kill you. Then researchers found out that it wasn't the hamburger at all! It was the bun they put it in that will kill you. Then we were told not to drink tap water. It has too many germs. It became a fad to drink Perrier mineral water from France. Who drinks French water? You can't get clean water from France. It's filthy! Even the French don't dare drink their own water. They drink wine. *USA Today* discovered that there are more germs in mineral water than there are in tap water. Even mineral water has an expiration date on it. What's going to happen if it exceeds the expiration date? Does it turn into tap water?

People are scared to enjoy what they eat. They read labels, weigh calories, and consult with experts. Tell me, is this living? Where's the old gusto to down a kishke with a ginger ale chaser? Even if eating "health food" would get me to live an extra year, who wants the extra year without a hot pastrami sandwich on rye with mustard and a side order of pickles and cole slaw? Brett Leake says: "I will start eating natural foods when people stop dying of natural deaths."

"Yeah, but if I don't get that extra year," I've heard people say, "I might not get to see my grandchildren." Has anybody ever done research on how many people would rather have a frozen vodka and roasted peanuts rather than waiting to see the grandchildren yet to be born?

It was the fad in the 1950s to smoke. Actors, lawyers, doctors all smoked, trying to be "in." Now everyone's hysterical about smoking. "Millions of people will die due to smoke related illnesses," is the present hype. Has anyone bothered to discover how many people will die who don't smoke? And why is there a label on cigarette packs warning, "Smoking may cause lung cancer", while on whiskey bottles there are no labels stating, "Booze may be hazardous to your relationships." Why aren't there labels on McDonald's hamburgers, or on tuna fish cans? Tuna fish may kill you.

Eventually, we learned that people who didn't smoke were dying of lung cancer. Of course, why not? We talk much today of second-hand smoke! Second-hand smoke may kill you! "She died of lung cancer. She didn't smoke, but her husband smoked. He killed her with his second-hand smoke. He's still alive and out there killing people!" Can you imagine what third-hand smoke may do to you? I empathize with people becoming anxious around smokers. Some prefer to eat pizza with Mozzarella cheese instead.

An elderly couple in their eighties, who had taken great care to eat proper and healthy foods, and who exercised all of their lives, died in a car accident. When they got to heaven, they were met by an angel, who immediately invited them to a banquet. When the couple saw what was being served, they refused, claiming that the food was full of fat and cholesterol.

"But you're all ready in heaven," the angel protested to them. "It doesn't matter what you eat." The elderly man looked at his wife.

"How much does all this cost?" he then inquired of the angel.

"Nothing," the angel replied, smiling. "You're in heaven now. And it's free!"

Suddenly saddened, the woman turned to her husband and began to cry.

"Oh, why did we have to eat healthy foods and exercise regularly all of our lives? We could have gotten here at least ten years ago!"

Deeply embedded in the Jewish psyche is the message: "Don't talk out loud about your fortunes." I acknowledge that Israel is the only country in the world where "today" is never good enough. "Tomorrow will be better," we constantly opine. And when tomorrow comes, you will hear the same recorded message, "It'll be okay." There are Israeli songs dedicated to waiting until next year to see how good it will be. Whenever I am confronted with that tired, old, "Everything will be okay," I respond, "If you can decide that everything will BE okay, what's your objection to deciding that everything IS OKAY NOW?" Their answer to that is usually, "Don't worry, everything will be okay."

And what about the songs on the radio that emphasize the past, such as, There Was a Time? I get the feeling that most Jews exist with one foot in the future, one foot in the past—and piss on *the present*! The Jew is forever waiting for something. It's in our DNA to wait for HaMoshiach (the Messiah).

It is so difficult for the average person to accept the here and now underlying the what is. Responses to the greeting, "How are you?" are usually, "Life sucks." Not only that, but you can also get a menu. We have "Life is crappy." or "The same old crap." My suggestion is that we all wait for HaMoshiach to come. Things are bound to get better then.

If you want to get my drift, listen carefully to the American National Anthem. It's full of power, hope, initiative and boldness. Then try listening to the lachrymose Israeli National Anthem, Hatikva. It's full of pathos, bathos, tragedy, and tearful pleading. We're just wired that way.

I once traveled to Istanbul with my Israeli brother-in-law, who warned me that Turkey was a Muslim country, and that we therefore must refrain from speaking Hebrew and laughing aloud in places so as not to draw attention to ourselves.

"Are you having fun?" he later asked me in the day, in all seriousness. My definition of a Jew is "someone who, the moment that he/she begins to feel good, will sit in the corner till the feeling passes."

Charlie Chaplin once said, "The difference between tragedy and comedy is distance." Up close, things seem tragic. Distance yourself from it and you get comedy. The formula for this concept is "T+T=C. Tragedy plus Time equals Comedy." The stories of our past, which were once so painful, when told today seem playful.

Prior to my eleventh birthday, no meat of any kind had ever passed between my lips. We were bordering on "poor." I ate corn flakes for breakfast, providing I didn't scrape the spoon across the plate and wake my mother up. That used to really piss her off. For lunch, I ate frozen potpie, which I learned to bake in the oven by myself, as both my parents worked. And for supper there were eggs, bread, and cheese.

The first time I ever saw meat on the table was when my sister got engaged and my mother invited her future son-in-law for a dinner. Of course, he had to be given the royal treatment. Thus, I had my first encounter with a lamb chop.

"Meat for dinner? Wow! What's going on here?" I innocently raved, as I felt my mother pinching me under the table.

Throughout the meal I kept on telling my future brother-in-law how happy I was that he was going to marry my sister so that I could eat lamb chops. My thigh was black and blue for a whole week from the pinching.

In order to be funny, I think that a person has to have had a screwed-up childhood. This qualifies most of us. Being funny does not necessarily mean knowing how to tell jokes. It means choosing to see humor and paradox as ways to deal with misery.

Besides, laughing burns up calories from overeating when you're unhappy. It's exercise at its easiest. You can even do it sitting down.

CHAPTER FIVE

Playing with Embarrassments

Optimism implies the courage to be imperfect.
—Martin E.P Seligman

Learning to laugh at our embarrassments has got to be the scariest thing in the world; especially when our bloopers are performed in front of other people. Humor and self-righteousness are mutually exclusive. True humor is laughter at oneself.

USA Today once published an article about the greatest fears of mankind and the order in which we express them. Everyone would normally think that the world's greatest fear is that of death. But the fear of death ranks second. The number one fear, even before death, is standing in front of an audience and speaking. That means that the person giving the eulogy at a funeral would rather trade places with the person in the coffin.

I think I could win a prize for the most embarrassing moments. I was once a radio and TV announcer. Being a broadcaster in the States meant that I had to learn to speak with a deep baritone or bass radio announcer's voice. Try to imagine my learning to say, in my resonant bass voice, "And now, back to our show, The Flying Chicken."

I had gotten so used to speaking in that cultivated voice that I found it a problem speaking any other way. "Hello, James. How's your family?" I might intone to a friend. Or I would find myself arriving home, announcing in my radio voice, "Hello, darling. Let's make love." I would also fantasize assuming an American *basso profundo* cadence for pornographic films, intoning "Oh! Oh! That's good! I'm coming! I'm coming!" as if reading the news.

Every evening, from Monday to Friday, exactly at eight, I would look at the camera, identify the red light that meant I was on the air and announce, "Good evening, and here is the news read to you by Leonard Ravich."

As usual, every morning I would arrive at the studio to open my mail. One morning, I noticed that someone had written my name on the envelope Leonard Rubbish instead of Leonard Ravich. It soon became epidemic. Letters were flooding in addressed to Leonard Garbage, Leonard Ravish (I'm innocent of any wrong doing.), Leonard Roberts, and even Leonard Rabbit. My ego was totally destroyed. I began searching my brain for a new last name, one that began with an "R." Robbins? Reynolds? I got it! Leonard Raymond. This would be my name from now on.

So the very next day, I arrived at the studio a bit early, in order to inform everyone that I had changed my name to Leonard Raymond. "Thank God," was the most common reaction. I took my place at my usual seat before the camera, waited for the red light to come on to announce, in my rich, broadcasting voice, "Good evening, and here is the news read to you by. . . ." But I couldn't remember the name I had chosen! My mouth went dry as I looked at the camera, trying to feign calmness while sweat poured from my forehead.

I tried again, "Good evening, and here is the news read to you by. . . ." By this time the cameraman was snickering and the soundman was doing his utmost to stifle his laughter. So I regained my composure, looked straight into the camera, and announced matter-of-factly, "I forgot my name, but here's the news:" I was devastated. Nothing went right after that. I was infamously known as the only announcer in the entire country who forgot his name during a live broadcast.

As luck would have it, things got even worse. When I arrived at the studio the next day, I sensed something was terribly wrong. The secretary, for the first time since I had made her acquaintance, was smiling at me. In the USA, when the secretary smiles at you, you have a very serious problem.

"The director wants to speak with you," she said almost giggling. At her words, my stomach immediately filled with lead and my heart leaped into my throat. I thought nervously to myself, "I've been chasing after Mr. Johnson for more than two months, trying to arrange a meeting with him. He never had time. And now—Oy, Vey!—he wants to speak with me?! Was I done for?" That's all I could think of.

I approached his office and got the first bad omen: the smell of coffee emanating from his room. In the States, when you're about to be fired, great care is taken to do it elegantly. Sometimes a catering company is invited to offer atmosphere. I entered his kingdom and saw it all: wall-to-wall carpeting, coffee, cakes, cigars. "The Last Supper," I thought to myself.

Mr. Johnson pointed to a chair and said, "Come in, Mr. Garbage, and take a seat." He then offered me, and I accepted, a cup of coffee and a chocolate cookie.

Now, it's important to note that I had never, ever, not once in my life, eaten a chocolate cookie without first dunking it in whatever I was drinking. As he was carrying on with small talk, I was trying to figure out how to dunk the cookie without his being aware of it. He finally turned to his desk and I quickly dunked the cookie. But then, I couldn't believe my eyes. Half of the cookie remained in my hand, while the other half was swimming and bobbing around in the coffee. It was like the half-cookie was looking at me, desperately pleading for me to rescue it from drowning to death.

A normal person would have put the cup of coffee and the half-cookie on the table and continued the small talk. But as I mentioned earlier, I carry my mother in my head, and I could clearly hear her demand, *"Finish everything on your plate! There are children in India who are starving!"* I would always confront her with, "If I finish all the food on my plate, how's that going to help the starving children in India?"

I tried tipping the cup toward my lips so that the soggy cookie would swim closer and then, like a vacuum cleaner, I would suck-slurp it in into my mouth, a trick I learned from my sister. But when I attempted to act on my idea, it suddenly occurred to me that there is a Murphy's Law concerning cups of coffee and abandoned soggy cookies. The law states: "The more you want the soggy cookie to come to you, the more the soggy cookie will try to avoid your advances."

So I protruded my upper lip to try to retrieve what was left of this once whole chocolate cookie, but to no avail. Upper lips were not made to complete such tasks. I tipped the cup straight up to offer the cookie one last chance to redeem itself. Nothing! By this time, the soggy cookie was clinging to the cup to save its dear life. And that's when Mr. Johnson elegantly declared, "Mr. Garbage. We're concerned with your welfare and have come to the conclusion that you will be much happier somewhere else."

By this time, I wasn't really listening, because I was wildly tapping the bottom of the cup, while holding it straight up to my mouth, determined with all my being to force that soggy cookie out of that cup and into where it belonged—in my mouth. Not having really heard Mr. Johnson (my mind was on rescuing the poor half cookie), I said, "Mr. Johnson, I'm quite satisfied here at the station, thank you." All of a sudden, the cookie took on a mind of its own, slid out of the cup and on to my shirt. Poor Mr. Johnson, he was more embarrassed for me than I was for myself.

What would it take for all of us to start telling other people about our most embarrassing moments with a bit of humor? It's frightening to even think about it; but I guarantee you, if we did this, we would not only feel better about ourselves, we would actually be stronger and more in control.

To verify what I am talking about, take your right arm and hold it stiffly to the side, while you think of yourself in a positive, successful light. As you do this, ask someone to try to pull your stiff arm down. Ask them to do it again while you think of yourself in a critical, judgmental light. Ask that person which time was easier to force your arm down. Invariably, it would be more difficult the first time, because when seeing ourselves as worthwhile beings empowers us emotionally as well as physically. Laughing at ourselves and seeing the humor in embarrassing settings will give us this power we need to live well.

While living in New York, and trying my fate as a theater director and actor, I was forced to support myself in between acting jobs (which was all the time) as a substitute teacher in the New York City school system. Although my license listed me as an English teacher, I got sucked into teaching physical education, math, health, and even a sewing class.

I was once asked to sub for an eighth grade math class. As it turned out, the regular teacher had broken her leg in a skiing accident and would be laid up for six weeks. As a result, I too, was in a tough spot—I hadn't the slightest idea how to teach a math class, even for one day. Now I would have to do it for six weeks!

The worst part of this dreadful situation stemmed from the fact that my students knew far more than I did and each day wound up catching me trying to fake it. I felt like the title character in the children's story *The Emperor's New Clothes*. However, in my case, it wasn't just the students who knew I was naked—but so did I. As a result, I spent every day of those six weeks in a constant state of humiliation. Thinking back on it, I was the one who learned far more than the students. If you're going to fake it, you sure as hell better be prepared to get caught at it, and to be ready to face the consequences.

No matter how we look at it, life is one huge, on-going improvisation. None of us gets an orientation manual when we're born, telling us how to handle every situation that might cross our path throughout our lifetime. Nor can our parents prepare us for every conceivable occurrence. Therefore, we are all improv actors, whether we want to be or not.

Here's an example of what I mean. One of the students in the math class, William Wong (I still remember his name.), caught me faking it for approximately the one-hundredth time. I immediately went into the self-defense mode and challenged him to teach the lesson himself. To my surprise, he agreed and proceeded to give a great lesson!

I understood nothing, but the children were inspired. Before the closing bell, I asked if someone else might be interested in teaching the next day's lesson. Twenty hands flew up, and I assigned the next day's lesson to another midget genius.

Since my challenge to Mr. Wong turned out to be a blessing in disguise (for me), I promised the class that I would continue this process on a daily basis as long as they behaved. Without a moment's hesitation, all of the students agreed to abide by my terms. I even assigned a student to design and correct the weekly quizzes. I would sit in the back of the class and try my best, to no avail, to decipher their explanations. They had no idea of my total bewilderment.

Whenever they got stuck, and turned to me for help, my answer to them was a very confident, "I'm sorry, but if I help you, you'll all become dependent on me, and a good teacher should never offer the answers to his students. You must solve this one yourselves." It must have worked, because they were as busy as ants while I sat in the back of the class revising my acting resume.

Gestalt therapists call this creative adjustment. Some people call it lying and cheating. But in my career as a student, I had to adjust creatively most of the time in order to pass some of my exams.

Based on my own experiences, here's an example of how creative adjustment works. In 1956, when the Russians sent Sputnik into space, our Navy's Admiral Hyman Rickover panicked. All of a sudden, America found itself behind in a race that it didn't even know it was in—the race to the moon.

Admiral Rickover concluded that we'd fallen behind because not enough science courses were being taught in our nation's schools. So, immediately, science courses became compulsory in every school in the country, universities included. There I was, two years into my college education, majoring in Theatre and English Literature and in order to graduate, I had to tackle a series of science courses. Can you imagine the responsibility that had been thrust upon my shoulders? The entire nation was counting on me to help it win the race to the moon.

As a result of having to study these courses (without any choice in the matter), I spent the entire semester suffering from nausea, headaches, and diarrhea. When it came time for the final examination in physics, I was in extreme blackout. This particular institute of higher learning happened to be a Baptist university and no one there ever cheated. They were taught, and sincerely believed, that Christ was in their hearts watching every move they made. How creative could I get, I wondered, in order to seduce a Baptist into giving me the answers to the exam?

I turned to this disgustingly bright, handsome student sitting on my left and asked, "Is it true that Christians are taught to help their fellow man?" He replied in the affirmative.

"Would it get you extra points with the Man Upstairs if you helped this particular fellow man?" Another affirmative. I got him to give me enough correct answers to get the hell out of that course alive.

When I handed in my exam, the professor glanced at it quite startled and inquired, "Where's the formula? You've got to have the formula." Would you believe that I went back and got the formula?

Why had I chosen to study at a Baptist university? Well, with my low grades from high school, no college in its right mind wanted to accept me. My one last try to a Baptist university was an appointment I had made with the President.

During our meeting, he explained that I had to have a certain grade point average in order to be admitted. He was sorry, but perhaps at some other time, after I had raised my grade scores, he would reconsider.

"Are you a Christian?" I asked, looking him squarely in the eye.

"Yes, of course," he responded, startled.

"If Christ were sitting right where you are now, would he grant me the privilege of studying here?" I slowly questioned him.

The rest is history.

After I graduated and left for Israel, I decided to go on for an M.A. My grades from college were so low that I was refused admission to study at Tel-Aviv University. I went back to the US, got my Master's, and went back to Israel only to be drafted as a lecturer at the very same university that had refused to accept me as a student. Looking back at these instances in my past allows me to conclude that a person with a sense of humor is one who witnesses constant paradoxes as a large part of his/her existence.

Creativity is humor. And humor is creativity. The elemental essence of creativity is the ability to see something that everyone else sees—from a different perspective. For example, if I handed you a pen and asked you to see a flute, would you be brave enough to take it to your lips and play *Yankee Doodle*? Or if I handed you a tennis racket, could you envision a banjo? Or a clothes hanger to be a bow and arrow? That's how children see the world.

Be as a child, and enter the kingdom of heaven.

Using creativity to tell people of embarrassing moments allows the magic of laughter to permeate the atmosphere, and when someone is laughing (true belly laughter and not nervous, embarrassed laughter), they can never be frightened or anxious. It is absolutely empowering during moments of stress. My greatest lessons have been learned while laughing at myself.

I once lived on a kibbutz where I was responsible for the chickens. Thousands of chickens were pampered there. Each one was allowed to live individually in her own cage, and was fed around the clock in order to produce as many quality eggs as possible.

Imagine my entering the chicken coop on a daily basis, putting their food onto a canal-type tray, while a thousand chickens stuck their heads out of their cages at the very same time and in the exact same manner, and quietly pecked away. Looking at this from the side gave the impression of a thousand soldiers lined up to be addressed. So I soon starting shouting, "Attention!" and watched as a thousand chicken heads came up at the very same time in total, unified shock. I loved it!

I made sure to arrive at the coop each day with a swagger stick under my arm as I played the British drill sergeant. I gave it a Cockney, "All right, girls. 'Oo wants to go 'ome? Attention!" and marveled at the power and control I had over my troops.

One day, I happened to look in the direction of the window and almost fainted. At least twenty kibbutz-niks were peeping in at me from the outside, with baffled expressions on their faces. Little did I know that each day someone would invite a friend to witness the spectacle by saying, "You saw the film *Dances With Wolves*? Well, come with me and I'll show you *Talks to Chickens*."

Now kibbutz-niks have the memories of elephants. They never forget. And once they get a victim, they are not likely to let up. Whenever I came into the dining room, there was a sudden silence. Then there would always be someone who couldn't hold it in any longer who would let out a snort-like chuckle, and this would bring the house down, with me standing there with egg on my face.

I remembered the magic of humor and realized that the only way out of this was *to learn to laugh with them at myself*. This required that I take an absurd stance by showing up in the dining room on Friday evening with the swagger stick under my arm. I chose Friday evening since this was the Sabbath and everyone was sure to be there wearing their finest festive clothing; even wearing shoes.

They didn't know whether to laugh or cry as I strutted around the dining room shouting, "Attention!" at every opportunity. I stopped at this one table where a group of super-critical diners were slowly sipping their soup. I took great relish in watching them spurt it out on the table while I gave them my "ATTENTION!" with extra effort.

When I turned sixty, I began to think I'd lost my sex appeal. One day, I got on a crowded bus heading for the center of Tel-Aviv. I paid my fare and as I turned to search for an empty seat, I suddenly noticed a lovely young girl smiling at me. I smiled back, anticipating an exciting encounter.

"I've still got it! She can't take her eyes off of me!" I said to myself.

She approached me with a very bright smile and inquired, "Would you like to sit down, sir? You can have my seat."

This ability to laugh at myself was made real for me in a film in which Charlie Chaplin plays a hobo who is so poor and hungry that he is forced to eat his shoe. It was ludicrous to watch as he elegantly cooked his shoe, put salt on it, taking great care to tuck a napkin under his chin, and slowly twirled the shoelaces around his fork like spaghetti. This combination of elegance and poverty taught me the value of laughing at myself and of putting my ego in my back pocket so that I could see the comedy in my own life. Laughing at one's own self is the greatest tool since the invention of the wheel.

I always carry a plastic spoon with me. Whenever I start taking myself too seriously, I take out the spoon, lick it and stick it on my nose. Whenever I get into an argument with someone, I hang the plastic spoon from my nose.

I am reminded of a remark made by Bernie Segal at a workshop I attended in the spring of 2001. He said, "Life is one big labor pain. We keep giving birth to ourselves over and over."

I would like to add, "And optimism and the ability to laugh at ourselves keep the pain from turning into tragedy. "

CHAPTER SIX

Spiritual Laughter

The world can be seen in two ways: Nothing is a miracle.
Everything is a miracle.

—Albert Einstein

Humor is spirituality and spirituality is humor. A wise, old Arab once proclaimed something about God being a humorist playing to an audience that's afraid to laugh. Once we all get to see this whole thing we call "life" as one huge cosmic joke, we have no other choice but to laugh.

In his book *Life After Life*, Thomas Moody, M.D. searches for and examines the reasons we are put here on this earth. Moody interviewed over seven hundred people who had a near-death experience. They had all been reported clinically dead and returned to life to tell about it. All of these people, all from different parts of the world, and none of whom knew one another, revealed the very same tale.

As their hearts stopped beating, they all found themselves floating out of their bodies, and, from above, were able to watch their bodies dying. They then felt an irresistible pull into a dark tunnel that eventually led them to a *being* surrounded by a blinding, white light. They all felt an incredible sense of well-being and unconditional love by this light. They all reported a feeling of complete peace and joy while this *being* asked them two questions:

How much have you learned to love?

How much have you used all the opportunities you had, while alive, to increase your wisdom?

They each then felt a powerful pull forcing them back into their bodies, where they were loathe to return, and regretfully felt that this was not their time to leave their bodies and part from this world, just yet.

While I am in no position to say whether Dr. Moody's results are valid or not, I do believe that the reason we were born into this world is to increase our capacity to love, and to expand our wisdom. I would like to add that having fun doing both of these would greatly enhance our success as human beings in relationships with other human beings.

I believe that's why we get married, have children, and start businesses. When we do all three of these things, we confront all the things in life that *don't work;* things that seem as if they are *not supposed to work.* We invite these events to appear in our lives so that we may see them as *opportunities to grow, to learn how to love more deeply, and to expand our wisdom.*

Poor is the one who tries to make life work. It's not supposed to work. It was placed in our midst to teach us, and it is our choice to have fun and laugh while learning, or go through the process in a state of constant frustration and desperation.

A woman participating in one of my humor workshops was asked why she had chosen to attend.

"Because I've been the victim all of my life," she informed the room. After the workshop, I questioned her once again.

"Have you now stopped feeling that you are the victim?" I inquired. We could all see that she was taking her time to consider the question for a moment.

"No," she offered confidently, "I'm still the victim. The difference now is—I enjoy it!"

A large part of the spiritual journey is looking at life as if everything and everyone was put on this earth to be our teacher, and that it's our responsibility to learn from them how to love more deeply and how to increase our wisdom. We are challenged to learn from the monsters that we invite into our lives, including our own selves.

A guy went to a therapist and said that the reason he was seeking therapy was that he felt like a dog.

"How long have you felt this way?" asked the intrigued shrink.

"Ever since I was a puppy," was the sincere reply.

My secretary works part-time for me and full-time as a bookkeeper in an office. She cried to me once that her supervisor had recommended that she be transferred to a different department and that his behavior towards her was nasty and revengeful. I advised her to look at this event as if her boss was sent to her by the powers above so that she could have the opportunity to love and become wiser.

"How can I possibly learn to love someone who tries to hurt me and take revenge on me?" she countered, declaring, "I'm going to get back at him if it's the last thing I do. I'll show him!"

"'Ha posel memamo posel'," I quoted from the Hebrew teachings: *The one who judges another also judges himself.*

I asked her to try to identify that part of his personality that she has difficulty in accepting in her own self.

"Once you learn to accept and even love that part in you that you are judging in him, it will be a lot easier for you to forgive and love him. As Rabbi Hillel in *Perkei Avot (The Sayings of the Fathers)* states, 'Love others as you love yourself'. See how you actually invited him and this situation into your life, because it's time for you to learn, to grow, and to move on." We both got out of our chairs and hugged. It was a powerful moment. The release of the tension caused us both to laugh.

Placing blame on others always reminds me of the story of the woman who complains to her rabbi that she cannot continue living with her husband.

"And why not?" the rabbi solicits?

"My husband thinks he's a refrigerator!" she exclaims in exasperation.

"So accept him as he is," the rabbi wisely cajoles.

"I can't!" she cries out, her frustration rising. "He sleeps with his mouth open, and the light bothers me!"

Today, I can say that I try not to give my power away by seeking revenge, as I had done in the past. I figure that feeling vindictive and unforgiving is a huge waste of time. I have found that love, optimism, and laughter are the most potent tools available to mankind.

Here is another example of the wise aphorism that *the one who judges another also judges himself*. I was once introduced to a man I could not tolerate on any level. He was loud, rich, and just plain gross. By the way, I find it rather interesting that we humans usually fail to recognize in ourselves those qualities that we find and dislike in other people.

At any rate, meeting this man for the very first time, I wondered, "*Why the strong physical reaction to this guy, Lenny? Why do I reject him so?*" In a split second I realized that I was confronting my own self. I was brought up to believe that only the poor are spiritual. You know: "The meek shall inherit the earth" type thing. But I was now suddenly observing that I was the photo and this man was my negative. Everything in nature is whole, and this person, as part of the whole, was offering me the opportunity to accept the "rich, loud, forceful" Lenny that I had for so long rejected and hidden.

By the time I had reached him across the room, instead of holding out my hand for him to shake, I opened my arms to welcome his embrace.

"You are my teacher. You are my *tikkun.*" I whispered in his ear, as I hugged him. In the wisdom teachings of the Jewish Qabbalah, when we repair a part of our life, this reparation is called a *tikkun.*

He hadn't the slightest idea what I was talking about, but he smiled anyway because I think he enjoyed the hug. Ever since that "lesson," I've allowed myself to make a lot more money. I love it. Money is very spiritual. I share it openly. The more I have and share, the closer I feel to God.

During the 1970s, I worked as a director in a theater and was once asked how I went about choosing a particular play to direct. My answer was that "if I walk out of the theater the same person I was when I walked in, then, for me, that play has no place in the repertoire." The play must have a profound effect on me, must change me in some way, and then it has a sporting chance to influence the audience.

After I made the decision to direct my first play, I decided that my selection of material should be something that would really offer me the opportunity to learn as much as I possibly could in my first attempt. I wanted something that would challenge me. So I chose Thornton Wilder's *Our Town*. Now, although this play is performed hundreds of times a year in countless amateur theaters in America, it is not an easy piece. In fact, it is a very difficult one. And not just for the actors, but even more so for the director. Let me explain.

What makes this classic play such a bear to pull off is the fact that it's missing the two ingredients that make for conflict (and what's a story without a conflict?); a protagonist and an antagonist do not exist. I told you, I wanted a challenge. The first act is called *Birth*, and it deals with that subject. The second act is called *Marriage*, and involves just that. The two main characters, childhood friends Emily and George, decide to get married in the second act. And yes, you guessed it. Act three is called *Death*.

In the third act, Emily dies while giving birth and is lowered into her grave. After her shocked reaction at meeting her old, dead relatives, she refuses to accept her death and proclaims that she wants to go back to life. She must! She has a little baby at home and has also purchased a brand new car. She is granted her wish to go back and join the living, but only on one condition. She is to choose a day from her past to re-live, and must never live forward into the future, since she has no future.

Emily agrees to the condition. She chooses her sixteenth birthday. Emily goes back to that time in the past, but as two characters. One character, a sixteen year-old, celebrating her birthday, and the other, as a person who has already died and is witnessing this same event from the side, with no chance either to renew or to change anything of her life, but only to view it as is.

Now wouldn't it be interesting if we were to play that make-believe game with ourselves once in a while and see our lives from the standpoint of two characters: as one character who experiences what is happening in *the here and now*, and as one who has already died and has chosen *this* day and *this* hour to come back and witness the same moment from the side? Things could appear differently then. Life could then even be comical.

Once in a while I've used that game that the Emily of *Our Town* gets to experience: being two characters at the same time, one who experiences life as it happens on a particular day and one who, in death, observes the chosen moment as a non-critical onlooker. For example, I was once invited to appear on a huge, prime time television program in Israel. I enthusiastically accepted. While waiting backstage to be introduced, I felt my body going into deep pain. What was it? Every cell in my body was on fire. I stood to the side and witnessed myself as Emily had done. One of my Me's was doing the experiencing while the other Me was watching from a distance, having died and chosen this day to re-live.

"My goodness, Lenny is scared," observed the witness part of me, who had already died and come back. It's a good thing the witness was focused at that moment, because I could never admit to fear.

"What are you frightened of? What's the worst possible thing that can happen?" the witness interrogated.

"I'll make a mistake, look foolish, and everyone will make fun of me and disrespect me," I revealed to this wise, old witness.

"What are you going to do with this fear?" he probed.

Then, looking up, I spoke to God.

"God, you're the one responsible for bringing me here. If I blunder, the blunder is all Yours. You are taking over from now on. So decide what You want to do."

And He/She did.

I went out on stage never so calm in my life, knowing that God had taken over—had assumed me—and does not like to make a *faux pas*. And if He/She does, who cares? I wasn't the one doing anything, anyway. God was doing through me. Lenny was the character God was now playing.

Perhaps the smartest person in the world is the one who is the most often quoted. Whenever I recall the experience of my momentary stage fright, I also remember one of my favorite gems from Anonymous: *The optimist sees the solution in no-solution, but only faith in the power of loving God.*

Let's return to *Our Town* for a moment. Emily, dead and, by choice, witnessing her life over again at her sixteenth birthday, is frustrated at her failure to communicate with the living, and requests that she be returned to her grave. But before her wish to return to her final resting place is granted, she begs for one last chance to say goodbye to the world before she separates permanently.

She pauses just before entering her burial place and laments:

> *Goodbye, world. Goodbye to Grover's Corners, to Mom and Dad. Goodbye to sleeping and waking up, to clocks ticking, to hot baths, to my cup of coffee and warm bun in the mornings. Oh, world, you're too wonderful for people to realize you when they're alive, every, every moment! Why don't people live their lives every, every moment?*

The answer comes rushing back to her—and to us—from the Stage Manager, who appears suddenly on the stage.

"Some do. Poets and Saints do, maybe, sometimes."

"People are so foolish not to live their lives every, every moment," she bitterly whispers, not satisfied with the Stage Manager's response, as she is lowered into her tomb.

Fade to black.

Think of that! To live life every, every moment, and to live each day as if it were our last! What would we like to do our last day on earth? Could we try to do what Emily asks of us, see life as a blessing and make each day holy by our giving thanks, each moment? Or would we live our lives as Emily did her life before she died?

Woody Allen has opined, "I'm not afraid of death. I just don't want to be there when it happens."

My mother used to say, "Live every day as if it's your last. One day you'll be right." I sincerely try to follow her advice.

Once, while my wife and I were vacationing in Turkey one summer, she suggested that we undertake a special excursion together.

"To where?" I asked.

"Pomukela," she offered.

"Where is that?" I inquired.

"Oh, it's a lovely place. Twelve hours by bus to get there and twelve hours back," she informed me innocently.

"I'm not interested," I insisted with determination.

"Why not?" she pursued.

"Because today is my last day, and I don't feel like dying on a bus." I admitted sincerely.

"Where do you prefer to die today, since it's your last one?" she caustically inquired.

"Sitting on the edge of the pool with a cold glass of beer," I proclaimed emphatically. "And if the Angel of Death doesn't tap me on the shoulder, I'm going to order another glass of cold beer!"

By the way, I've been married for thirty-five years. I'm still in love with the same woman for thirty-five years, and if my wife finds out who she is, she'll kill her and me.

Recognizing our spiritual side means being able to tell the difference between the noise (the shoulds and should nots) in our head and the wise voice deep inside us, our inner guide, that is.

On November 5, 1965, I was a single man teaching English in high school in Eilat (Israel's most southern border on the Red Sea). It was on that momentous day that I heard or felt a voice telling me that my wife was at the beach waiting for me.

"*Crazy*," I tell myself.

This voice in my head is ridiculous; a hallucination, at the least. Yet despite these feelings about the inner voice in my head, or the feeling in my gut, I felt compelled to listen—and listen—and off to the beach I went. After all, what was the worst that could happen? A little sun and comfort from the near-winter warmth?

I sat on the edge of the Red Sea waiting for my next instruction.

I watched as two Swedish beauties came laughingly out of the sea. I asked myself whether one of them could be she?

"Don't get excited by these two," the wise voice of my guide (God?) reacted. "Your wife is a native born Israeli." This is becoming absurd. That wise voice (God?) even knows her nationality?

So I shut up and waited. Then I heard her voice. She was explaining to some traveler from Canada, in English, how to get to a particular kibbutz in the North.

"*That's her!*" Something said.

So I walked over to her and the rest is history. We were married six weeks later, December 21, 1965.

I invited my mother, who had been living in the USA at the time, to my wedding. My mother, who spoke Yiddish, thought that every Jew in the world is familiar with Yiddish. My wife's parents are from the Spanish heritage. When my mother spoke to my wife's parents in Yiddish, they answered her in Ladino, the language of the Marranos, the Jews who were expelled from Spain in 1492. My mother, shocked from this discovery, whispered in my ear, "Why didn't you tell me you were marrying a shikse" (A non-Jewish woman)?!

I have found that when I am connected to the wise, holy voice within (God), which always happens when I care enough to recall that I am constantly attuned to the Holy Spirit, I feel a rush of well-being and joy. Whenever I forget this holy connection and begin listening to the shoulds and the should nots in my head (incoherent noise telling me what I *should or should not* do rather than what I want or *need* to do), I feel weak and sometimes suffer pains in my body.

To feel energized, all I have to do is concentrate on the feeling deep inside and stay in touch with what my next thought or action will be out of honor for the holy voice and guidance I am receiving at that moment. I truly believe that we all have access to this powerful God and well-being within, once we choose to listen, feel, and differentiate the holy voice within from the intrusive noise within.

A man heard his inner voice telling him to sell his house, his car, and his business, and to go to Las Vegas. He tried his best to avoid hearing this, since he spent much energy and many years accumulating his small fortune. The inner voice persisted day and night, "Sell your house, your car, your business and go to Las Vegas."

Finally, not being able to tolerate it any longer, he obeyed. He sold everything and went to Las Vegas. The moment he arrived in Las Vegas, he heard the inner voice once again, ordering him to immediately go to Caesar's Palace. When he entered the casino in Caesar's Palace, he heard the voice once again. "Walk over to the roulette wheel. Put all your money on red twenty-three." He obeyed. The wheel spun around and around and stopped at—seventeen black. At first there was a deafening silence, and then the inner voice said— "Damn!!"

When I was a teacher in high school, I would approach every student who gave me a difficult time and whisper in his ear, "Thank you for coming into my life. I must have invited you, because you have been my *tikkun.*

In the Jewish religion, laughter is highly respected. We even have, as one of our Fathers, a holy man named Laughter (Yitzchak; Isaac, in English). He received that name because his mother, Sarah, laughed when she had heard from the angel that she was to give birth at the age of ninety. It's a good thing she didn't burp!

I have come to the conclusion that life is a terminal disease. Live every day as if it were our last, because someday we'll be right. As Ram Dass has said about life: "We can drag it or we can dance it." Those are the choices.

One morning I got up and realized that my wife was in the bathroom vomiting. She looked terrible. She had dark circles under her eyes and her skin was covered with sweat. I quickly grabbed her in my arms, put her gently in the car, and immediately took off for the hospital. As I began to drive, my wife started moaning from pain and nausea. In order to distract her from the discomfort, I instantly started to entertain her with jokes and funny stories.

She stared at me with her pained eyes (Were my jokes that bad?).

"Why are you trying to make laugh? Can't you see I'm not well?" she complained.

"I want to make sure that if you die, at least you'll greet the Angel of Death with a smile." I deflected.

"It's true. I might die!" she blurted out through her pain.

She then seemed to hesitate, and then her eyes filled up with tears.

"Lenny, promise me that if I die, you'll marry a good woman to look after our children." She advised me softly.

"Baby, when you die, you've got no control over what I do," I advised in return, with my eyes glued to the road. "There are no remote control devices in the grave. I will choose any woman I want to with no consultation from you!"

Pulling herself up a bit, she looked straight ahead and demanded, "Turn the car around. I'm not going to any hospital!"

It was amazing how the healthy color immediately returned to her face.

As I will always exclaim, "Every thought is a prayer."

CHAPTER SEVEN

Emotional Laughter

Be in touch with feelings. Don't hide the pain.
—Lenny Ravich

It's amazing, when we think about all the courses we have sat through, and subjects we learned in school and college, that none of them had to do with feelings. We received diplomas and certificates to begin our careers, but not a single course on how to be an emotionally intelligent human being. Then we married, and eventually had children, without the slightest clue as to what to do regarding the emotions of others and our own.

A guy comes home and catches his wife in bed with another man.

"What are you doing home so early?" she shockingly asks.

"What are you doing in bed with another man?" he angrily demands.

"Don't change the subject!" she quickly responds.

Even at home, the best we often seem able to do with our affections is to hide them. In my family, feelings were considered a weakness.

"I'll give you something to cry about!" is how I was dismissed whenever I cried. So I was taught that being a man meant hiding sadness, demonstrating toughness.

Fear was also considered a threat to manhood. "C'mon, you can handle that. What are you, a baby?!"

It wasn't until later that I discovered that a man who is not afraid of his wife is not a real man.

I'm reminded of the story of the wife who chases her husband around the house with a broom, trying to beat him with it, only to find him hiding under the table.

"Come out from under there so I can take a good crack at you!" she shouts.

"I'm the man in this house! I alone decide when I come out!" he shouts back, even more loudly.

Anger was looked upon as primitive when I was growing up. "Don't you dare talk to me in that tone of voice. What are you, some kind of animal?"

Even happiness was met with, "What are you so excited about? Calm down!"

I don't think I'm an exception. Most men are not given permission to have emotions. Most of us express everything through violence—be it words or actions. Women are forced into a dilemma because of the way we use words on them.

Seemingly, women are allowed all feelings available, except their very own anger. That's why many women cry when they get mad. God forbid a woman should express her anger. Then she's considered either a "controlling bitch" ("She always cries and bawls to get me to do things her way!") or, at best, a "mindless puppy" ("Ahh, you're so cute when you get angry."). In either case, words are the man's weapons of destruction.

Feelings, if we ever get permission to have them, are our truth.

A man went to a therapist. "I want to find the real me," he pleaded.

"That's no problem," the therapist informed the man. "Come once a week. It'll cost you $150 an hour."

"Find the real *me* and get *him* to pay you," the man huffed.

Women want to know why some men are so closed. Most of the time we men feel like turtles in a hailstorm. We experience being constantly criticized, and have difficulty expressing ourselves. It's even hard for us to say, "I love you."

Feelings are who we are. They signal what we need. When we know what we feel, we know what we need. Then we can start looking for ways to get those needs satisfied. Was there anyone during our young lives who taught us this tremendous lesson in survival? I doubt it.

A man went to a party with his wife and began dancing with other women there. His wife, approaching him, declared, "You've danced with every woman here but me. When are you going to ask me to dance?"

He laughed. "You? You dance like a washing machine."

After they returned home later on that evening, he tried to get intimate with her. "What?! For one rag, you expect me to start up the whole machine?" she exclaimed.

He is presently doing his own laundry himself by hand.

It needs to be said very emphatically that *we all subconsciously desire recognition, attention, love, and warmth.* Most of us were never taught how consciously to ask for them gracefully. When I used to ask for love, my request was met with disgust or with shock at having the "chutzpa" to even invite the thought. So I learned, like most of us, to manipulate people to give me what I needed. It was too dangerous to be vulnerable and open. When I got married, the only way I would allow myself to court my wife for some warmth or for sex was to play a bad mood. I would come home from work, slam the door, go to my room, and sulk. All this was done instead of saying, "Give me a hug, Hon." Or, "I'd really like to make love with you tonight."

When my daughter was a nine-year old, she spent many a day breaking dishes and then asking forgiveness. Every day another cup or dish bit the dust. One day I said, "Orite, just before you go to break another dish, come over to me and ask for a hug instead." She liked the idea. She stopped breaking dishes, but she became a tremendous nudnik for hugs.

Why do we manipulate, get stuck, mess up relationships?

Why do we hear questions such as, "Why does it always happen to me?" Or other such questions.

"Why is it that I always meet the wrong men?"

"Why is it that women always end up leaving me?"

"Why do I always end relationships in anger?"

"Why are the men I have relationships with always violent?"

Let's consider the following tale and see whether we can find some answers there to these introspective questions.

> *Once upon a time there was a pregnant fly.*
>
> *Just before she was about to lay her eggs, she saw a female dog giving birth. "How beautiful!" she thought to herself. "The moment her puppies will be born, she'll greet them into this world by licking them. They will search for her nipples and find all the milk they need to sustain them. They will sleep by their mother's side, knowing warmth and safety, gently listening to her heart beat while she lay there, hardly ever moving, constantly serving, except to relieve herself now and then. She won't even attend in-service training courses. I must do the same for my little ones. I won't be able to be there for them so I must at least find a place to lay my eggs where they will have enough food, warmth and safety. No less than those little puppies," she thought.*
>
> *So she searched and she searched and at last she found the ideal place. What do you think she found? Yes. A pile of shit. She laid her eggs in this pile of waste, knowing her offspring would find warmth, safety, and food. Then she flew away.*
>
> *The eggs, encouraged by the warmth from the manure, soon hatched. And the first thing these little maggots encountered upon being hatched was shit. They ate, they played, and they threw crap at each other for recreation, and behold, one day they began to sprout wings.*
>
> *They began to fly. They flew and they flew, but there was only one thing that would constantly attract their attention. The one thing they could never resist. Yes. "Cocky"! You see, this crap was familiar to them. The word "familiar" comes from*

the word "family." We're all attracted to and can't resist the
familiar "family crap."

How does this story apply to us?

Why is it that we keep going back to the same old crap?

We seem to choose the same bad inherited familial relationships and situations time and time again. My belief is that we marry and befriend those who will not, nor cannot, give us what we need. We marry them and befriend them in order not to get what we need. This sounds paradoxical, but remember, without the wisdom of the absurd, there is no funniness.

"How do we get out of it?" is the question I'm mostly asked. Well, to deal with this, we ought to have a sense of humor. In this case, we must not, heaven forbid, take ourselves too seriously—because there is no way out!

Because there is no way out, the best way "out" is to go "way in"
and laugh at ourselves. The more we try to change, the more we stay the same. The more we stay the same, with a sense of humor and the ability to laugh at ourselves, the more we change. Watching ourselves falling into these familiar familial, destructive patterns, and learning to laugh about it all, offers us the opportunity to accept, laugh at, and love ourselves with much compassion for self. That's the way toward and into change.

As Anne Teachworth always notes, change doesn't begin until we can fully see the absurdity of how we've co-created our own unhappiness and continued to justify living out the same bad scripts. Personal history repeats itself, Anne insists, unless we change our Inner Couple family imprint. In her book, *Why We Pick the Mates We Do*, she explains how to correct selecting mismatching, interactional patterns. We're in trouble, she points out, when looking for our mate, we come across our (family-imprinted) *match* instead.

As my dear friend and colleague, Dina, jokes, "I love men—who leave me. If they were to stay in a relationship with me, I'd have to be intimate, and I couldn't handle that."

When I was in therapy, my relationship to my wife took

foreground in many of my weekly sessions. My therapist recommended that I bring my wife to one of our meetings. Of course, my wife refused, concluding that it wouldn't help. She should know. She's a psychiatric social worker.

Finally, and quite suddenly, my wife agreed to go with me. We arrived for the appointment ten minutes early. I started to get out of the car. My wife, however, wasn't budging. Somewhere between leaving home and arriving here, she had done a complete turnabout.

Changing her mind, she had not only refused to see my therapist, but clearly wouldn't even get out of the car. Why had she agreed in the first place? Did she placate me for the given moment; yet knew that when the final moment came, she would be unable to go through with it?

I immediately started to feel as if I were in a "for real, bad" Italian movie. We spent the next ten minutes simultaneously screaming, blaming, accusing, and denying. To this day, I'm not sure either of us heard what the other was saying. But it certainly was dramatic!

Suddenly, and without any explanation, she stopped screaming and marched into the therapist's office. We began the session and amazingly did a complete turnabout of our own this time, from our Felliniesque scene in the car. We talked calmly, tried to relate to one another, and for the most part did pretty well with our communication.

The following week, during my usual session, my therapist brought out the point that when I'm without my wife, I'm a pretty impressive figure; smiling, laughing, and quite sure of myself. She had observed that when I'm in my wife's presence, I'm more reticent, moody, placating, smaller, and compliant. Upon arriving home, I shared my therapist's observation with my wife. She walked over to me and stood with her legs about twelve inches apart, with her hands on her hips.

"Bullshit!" she screeched.

I looked her right square in the eye. "Okay!" I announced finally, and shrank back into my turtle shell.

That crap is certainly familiar in my life.

What parable can humor give us to help us understand such crap?

A man who had died and gone to heaven noticed that there were two lines approaching the Pearly Gates. One line was designated for "All the real men who had control over their wives." The other line was expressly for "Those men who feared their wives." The "fearful" line was packed nose to nose; so he walked over to the "real men" line, which was virtually empty, and waited.

An angel flew over to him and gently explained to the man that this was his last chance to tell the truth, and that the truth was absolutely critical in being accepted into the holy halls.

"Why have you decided to wait in this line?" the angel asked. "Everyone knows the reality of relationships between men and women."

"My wife sent me," the man meekly replied.

Using humor in fearful situations hands us the reigns over the situation. While we are laughing, we cannot be afraid. This has been checked out. Few people who laugh also develop ulcers. You can check that one out, if you want to.

I was visiting my sister during her daughter's sixth birthday. Shortly after being put to bed, my niece came storming out of her room.

"There's a man in my closet!" she screamed at her mother. My sister and I both accompanied my niece back to the room and opened the closet so that she could see that there was no man there. She soon went back to sleep, only to come out crying again.

"There's a man in my closet and I'm all alone!" she insisted.

"You're not alone," I explained. "There's a man in your closet to keep you company." She laughed and went back to sleep peacefully for the rest of the night.

Humor is a "must" for our survival kit. All of us have suffered criticisms, judgments, and comparisons. The most frequent feelings a lot of us have are those of being insufficient and unnecessary.

"I watched the sunset last night and felt so insignificant. Today it rained and I felt the same way," Woody Allen once admitted.

I gave a lecture last year to a group of retired doctors and their spouses. It was an absolute catastrophe. People were walking out in the middle, talking on their cellular telephones, and looked, for the most part, disinterested. The agent who had invited me asked me if I would please finish quickly and go home. I felt poisoned and degraded.

While driving home, I realized that I couldn't help flagellating myself over the miserable failure I just suffered. Then I took a deep breath and remembered who I am. I'm that guy who teaches people to survive by using humor. I suddenly remembered that just because I was talking negatively to myself doesn't make it so.

I began to laugh out loud. I drove around for about three miles, laughing all the while. When I finally stopped laughing, I forced myself to laugh again, knowing that my making myself laugh, even if I didn't much want to, would cause me to feel better and more in control.

"Fake it 'till you make it," I like to tell myself. A night like this would have, in the past, influenced me negatively for two weeks. I don't take myself too seriously any more; so when I tell this story I usually add, "This time it only took fourteen days." In fact, I did get over the unpleasantness more quickly after laughing about it. Even when I'm down, I act "as if" I'm happy. It works. When I think of something negative these days, I say to myself loudly, "Stop!" This works for me.

I have discovered that it's not what people say to us that makes us feel bad. It's what we say to ourselves after they have long gone that turns the wheels of the negative cycle. It's what we carry around with us in our imagination that can numb us to our feelings.

As Martin E.P. Seligman has observed in *Learned Optimism*, "The things we say to ourselves when trouble strikes can be just as baseless as the ravings of a drunk on the street. Changing the destructive things you say to yourself when you experience the setbacks that life deals all of us is the central skill of optimism."

I'm reminded of the story of the two rabbis racing to get to a minyan (the minimum of ten men required for afternoon prayer) in Jerusalem during a harsh rainstorm. They observed a young lady who was desperately trying to cross the street but was unable to because of the severe flooding. The older rabbi approached the young woman, took her in his arms, and brought her to safety.

Ten minutes later, as the two rabbis continued their journey in the rain, the young rabbi, who was beside himself with agitation, couldn't contain himself any longer.

"Rabbi," he addressed the older man," you know as well as I that the mere touching of a female is absolutely forbidden in our religion. Yet you chose to hold a young woman in your arms! Why?"

The older rabbi replied, "I left her there, but you're still carrying her around in your head."

What are we carrying around in our heads? Can we change the noise we get from the familial, embedded messages in our heads and plug into a higher level of understanding and compassion for ourselves? What prevents us from accepting ourselves unconditionally? All we need to be doing on this earth is to learn and to love. All the rest is technical. Is a life without criticism, judgment, and comparison possible? I think it is.

An anecdote is often told of a certain psychologist, B.F. Skinner, who experimented with torpedoes during the Second World War. It seems that the torpedoes used by the American Navy were missing their mark. Through his research, Skinner discovered that by teaching pigeons to peck at a picture of a ship, while receiving a pellet of food for each correct peck, he could alter their behavior enough so that they became interested in nothing more than pecking at the picture and eating their just deserts.

These pigeons were placed in a torpedo with a window at its nose. When the torpedo was fired, the pigeons could view the ship clearly from the nose of the torpedo and peck away at what they thought was a picture, which guided the explosive to its destiny.

We are the same. The unconscious mind is like a smart bomb. Whatever picture we see in our heads and persist in pecking away at, our subconscious will make sure to bring us to that very same destiny. Whatever we fear might come true will come true. If we change that fear to hope and love, whatever we hope for and love will have a chance to be realized.

Here are some ways in which we can learn to handle emotions optimistically:

1. Any emotion you have signals a need. If you feel angry, afraid, or sad—stop. Now take a deep breath and ask yourself, "What do I need right now?" Try to get that need satisfied, even if it requires asking for help in doing it. Ask for things. Ask for hugs. Enjoy life!

2. When you catch yourself saying cruel things to yourself, think, "There goes the noise in my head." Quickly say, "I cancel that thought. Stop!" Put a good, positive thought in its place. Say nice things to yourself. Stand in front of a mirror. Give yourself a compliment. Anything. Even "I want to compliment you on getting to work on time today." Then say, "I love you," straight into the mirror. This is not easy. It takes practice.

3. Knowing that a negative thought brings negative feelings and behavior, do not allow negative thoughts into your existence. Practice saying, "Thank you, God, for love, laughter, and good health." Don't spend your life doing what you don't want to do.

4. Upon meeting people, see only the positive side of them. Give compliments. Smile a lot. "Fake it till you make it." What you give you get back in return.

5. Use pain and fear to guide you. Move away from things and people you don't like being around.

6. Live all experiences in the moment.

7. Laugh at yourself, to yourself, and with other people as much as you can.

CHAPTER EIGHT

Healthy Laughter

Optimists seem to lead longer and healthier lives.
—Martin E.P. Seligman

Norman Cousins, author of the best selling *Anatomy of an Illness*, was diagnosed as having a terminal disease called *Ankylosing Spondylitis*. Chances for surviving its onslaught were slim at best. He was advised to check into the hospital but, instead, he ordered a room at a hotel and brought with him videotapes of The Marx Brothers, *Candid Camera*, Charlie Chaplin, Bill Cosby, Bugs Bunny cartoons, and anything else that would cause him to laugh. He believed that having a good laugh would help him feel better.

As he noted in his book, ten minutes of belly laughter allowed him two hours of painless sleep. His findings took doctors by surprise and medical researchers had a new subject to pursue. At the end of his experiment, Mr. Cousins was diagnosed as cured. Modern medicine proclaimed his cure a miracle.

As a precaution, Cousins returned to the hospital on a daily basis so that his urine could be examined. Before the nurse came by to pick up his urine sample, Norman put apple juice into the urine cup instead. When the nurse arrived, he studied the cup of liquid pensively.

"This looks rather cloudy," he suggested, just before he handed the cup to her. "I think I'll run it through again," he concluded, and proceeded to drink the juice from the urine cup. This sent the nurse out of the room screaming.

Researchers have discovered that when we laugh, the body releases endorphins, which is nature's way of killing pain. When these endorphins are released into the brain, a feeling of euphoria can exist for as long as two hours.

The doctor briskly enters the patient's room. "I have good news and bad news for you. Which would you like first?"

"Give me the good news first, Doc," the patient suggests cautiously.

"Well, you have forty-eight hours left to live."

"That's the good news? What's the bad news?"

"I forgot to inform you yesterday."

Madelon Visintainer (1990) became the first person to demonstrate that a psychological state of learned helplessness and pessimism can cause cancer. Laughter and joy cannot enter a helpless, pessimistic spirit.

Doctors have learned that laughter takes over the body like inner jogging. Our blood pressure rises momentarily with laughter and then drops below the level it was before the laughter. Medical people are now beginning to realize that a person who is ill, but who has an optimistic attitude and is humorous and takes time to laugh, has a 65% better chance of achieving a faster and more complete recovery. This is opposed to persons with a negative attitude, who also take things too seriously and lack even a modicum of humor, even about themselves.

In other words, try stepping out of the frame. Take a good look at the picture and find the humor in your self-portrait. In many hospitals in the States, humor and laughter have become a major factor in training courses for medical staffs. Joy is the preferred state of health.

The doctor briskly enters the patient's room. "I have good news and bad news for you. Which would you like first?"

"Give me the bad news first, Doc."

"You have Alzheimer's disease."

"That's tragic! What good news could you possibly have?"

"In another half-hour, you'll completely forget this conversation."

When we laugh, we push air into our lungs and out at the speed of 65 miles an hour, thereby cleansing our lungs and throat. Ten minutes of laughter is apparently worth one hour of zazen meditation, which has the same effect and result on our bodies.

Tears of laughter, because they are the result of laughter and joy as a cathartic action, cleanse the soul. Tears of sadness are also cathartic. Tears of sadness and tears of laughter come from the same source. Truly, as the Yiddish proverb teaches, "Soap is to the skin as laughter is to the soul."

One afternoon, I paid a visit to a nearby Kupat Holim; that is, a clinic for the ill, as we literally say in Hebrew. I asked the nurse at the reception desk whether I might have a word with the doctor. Phoning him from her post, she announced my arrival: "Doctor, your sick one is here."

When I heard her refer to me as the "sick one", I immediately bent over, feeling very sick and very old. She must know something that I don't, I thought. She's a nurse, after all. She noticed my body language and asked me whether everything was all right.

I pleaded with her to call the doctor back and tell him that his healthy one would like to talk with him. I told her that I would feel much better if she would do that. She explained that she couldn't do that since this was a Clinic for the Sick. She meant, of course, that even if I were healthy, the requirement for visiting a kupat holim was first and foremost to feel sick. In America, we have hospitals, which immediately implies hospitality. In Israel, we have, houses for the sick, from the Hebrew *beit holim*.

Laughter produces muscle relaxation, which reduces levels of stress hormones in the blood, thereby enhancing the immune system. Thoughts, moods, emotions, and attitudes have been shown to influence the body's basic health and healing mechanisms. Humor and laughter offer an effective means of assuring joy, good health, and well-being.

When I was fifty-seven years old, my cardiologist recommended that I undergo angioplasty. I asked the doctor straight out, "If I asked you to hug me, would you agree?" He laughed and said, "Yes, of course." When I undergo something as medically threatening as this, I want a human being as well as a doctor near me. His answer and his laughter convinced me that he was the person for the job. You don't have to be a doctor to heal people.

Hospitals have become convinced of the therapeutic power of humor. The humor-in-hospitals movement has also gained support because of the trend toward depersonalization in hospitals. Patients want a more personalized relationship with caregivers. I truly believe that a good connection and relationship with the hospital staff would keep us alive longer. Humor and optimism help establish it.

Among patients with heart disease, those with a pessimistic outlook about their ability to recover are more than twice as likely as optimists to die one year later.

Joseph Billings, M.D., once said: "There's no fun in medicine, but there is medicine in fun."

The seventeenth-century French philosopher Voltaire once said, "The art of medicine consists in keeping the patient amused while nature heals the disease."

Oncology units in hospitals have become interested in humor as a form of therapy. Cancer patients in the USA are now learning to improve their sense of humor as a means of bringing an additional weapon to fight against their disease.

Bernie Segal, M.D., once said, "The simple truth is that happy people generally don't get sick."

A man went to his doctor with a complaint about terrible headaches.

"There is only one solution. Castration," the doctor informed the man, after concluding his tests. The man was so desperate that he agreed to the operation. The operation was a success and his headaches had lifted.

He was so excited about his novel life that he went out to get fitted for new clothes.

"What size underwear do you normally wear?" the tailor asked.

Why, I wear a size 40," the man replied, puzzled. "Why do you ask?"

"Oh, no, you're at least a 44. You should never wear a size 40," the tailor advised. "Underwear that tight will cause you to have headaches."

The longer negative states persist in your mind/body, the greater the likelihood they will lead to some negative influence on your health.

A sign in a doctor's office: "Alzheimer patients must pay in advance."

Auschwitz death camp survivor Victor Frankl has observed in his Man's Search for Meaning that he used humor to keep him going through the daily horrors of the camp: "I never would have made it if I could not have laughed. Laughing lifted me momentarily out of this horrible situation, just enough to make it livable, survivable."

Frankl states that he and another prisoner tried to invent at least one funny story or joke every day.

"I'm glad that Hitler came to power," his fellow prisoner joked one evening, while warming their hands over a fire. "You were my neighbor for years and I never even spoke to you. Now, because of Hitler's rise to power, I have had the pleasure of getting to know you."

One day, this very same comical prisoner came to Frankl and blurted, "I had this terrible nightmare that I was in this concentration camp with thousands of starving and dying prisoners. Was I glad to finally wake up from that terrible dream and find myself in a concentration camp with thousands of starving and dying prisoners!"

Frankl once pointed to a capo (a fellow Jew now acting as a guard for the Nazis) and said, "Imagine, I knew him when he was just a mere bank president."

Mental patients who can learn to laugh at themselves are considered cured.

A recorded message at a psychiatric clinic presents the following instructions to callers:

"Hello, you have reached the psychiatric clinic.

"If you are obsessive-compulsive, please press #1 repeatedly.

"If you are co-dependent, have someone press #2 for you.

"If you are paranoid, we know who you are. Stay on the line so that we can trace this call.

"If you suffer from multiple personality disorder, press #3, #4, and #5.

"If you are suffering from a schizophrenic personality disorder, wait for a voice to tell you which number to press.

"If you suffer from clinical depression, it makes no difference what number you press, nothing will help."

AIDS patients with a more optimistic outlook have also been shown to survive longer, as have men suffering heart attacks. A sense of humor helps maintain this positive focus on a day-to-day basis.

A couple arrived to the doctor's office.

"How can I help you?" the doctor asked. The couple immediately stripped off their clothes and began to have sexual relations. After they finished—and finish they did!—they got dressed and sat down again in front of the doctor.

"I don't understand how you imagine you need my help," the perplexed doctor admitted.

"Oh, you have already helped!" offered the gentleman. "Do you know how much a hotel would have cost us in this town?"

In my workshops on humor, optimism, and laughter, I teach people to laugh artificially, even if they don't feel like it. We don't wait to feel good to laugh. We laugh in order to feel good. We take responsibility for our own well-being and don't postpone *joy*.

Once people force themselves to laugh, the chest's diaphragm, a muscle used in laughing, gets a workout. In time, it's much easier to slide into a laughing and joyful mode of being. My workshop participants' homework is to laugh for 15 seconds per day, twice a day. They can do it in their homes, in their cars, at work, or on the toilet. Humor Project originator Joel Goodman, of Saratoga Springs, New York, puts it this way: "They learn to laugh *jest* for the health of it."

My wife deals with stress by not watching the news. She videotapes the news. This is absolutely true. She watches the video-taped version of the news at a later date and declares, "Wow! I'm certainly glad that's over."

Upon arriving at his doctor's office, a man requested of the physician, "Doctor, please don't laugh at me when I show you my problem."

The doctor, who took an oath to do no harm, assured him that he was strictly professional and would certainly not laugh. The man pulled down his pants, and then his underwear, and lifted one of his testicles (the size of a bowling ball) on the doctor's desk.

The doctor erupted in laughter.

The disappointed man grumbled, "Because you laughed, Doc, I'm not going to show you the big one!"

Learning to see the funny side of things, including learning to laugh even when one doesn't feel like it, can become habitual, just like anything else. All we need is the conscious desire. Being too serious could and does cause us damage. Humor and laughter can save our lives.

"Laughter is always the best medicine," my grandmother would say.

Now doctors are doing research on laughter to find out whether my grandmother was right.

CHAPTER NINE

Humor and Growing Older

I always thought that getting old is what happens to other people.

—George Carlin

"Midlife has hit you when you stand in front of a mirror and see your rear end without turning around," Anonymous warns us.

The great American comic George Burns once opined, "You can't help getting older, but you can help getting old." I, too, believe that looking at getting older with humor is a miraculous opportunity to laugh at ourselves and stay young at heart.

I'm writing this book at the age of sixty-four. If I decided to write my first book at this age, how can anyone say that it's too late to do something? Whenever I think it's too late to undertake something new, I ask myself, "How old will I be if I don't do it?"

Thank God I can still dance. It's getting in and out of the car that's a real bummer. When I start dancing, I have no age at all, and I'm the last one to leave the dance floor. I can go on all night. My wife is the same.

On the other hand, someone once said," You are as young as you feel." This may be true, but getting my socks on in the morning has become a major project.

I spent twenty-three years working as a supervisor for the Board of Education. I went out on early retirement at the age of sixty. Ever since my retirement, I've had nightmares. I keep dreaming that I return to work.

But I've become seriously busy since retirement. The difference between working before retirement and afterwards is that I used to draw a salary. I now, however, make money. I do what I truly love and I do it *with my whole heart*, which, I believe, keeps me young.

My first shock concerning my age was at the age of thirty-nine.

I went to purchase a bathing suit. I chose a bikini because that's what I had worn till then. The new one I had chosen didn't fit, however.

The storeowner let me try on boxer trunks similar to what my grandfather had worn. And that's exactly what I saw when I looked in the mirror: a grandfather! I was depressed.

For the first time in my life, I looked at the mirror and saw a bulging belly, and fat on my hips! I thought I was looking at myself in a mirror at the "house of fun" of an amusement park.

It wasn't funny then, but looking back on it is. At my age, being around beautiful women is like a child being in a chocolate factory with his mouth-taped shut.

Getting older is relative.

I went to a medical clinic for a check-up one day and noticed a woman in her seventies looking very pale and moaning and crying. I asked her what was wrong.

"I'm desperate! My doctor is on vacation," she sniffed.

"You don't need a doctor. You need a big hug," I smiled.

The color suddenly started to return to her face.

"A hug? From a young man like you?" she blushed.

I simply wrapped my arms around her and hugged her for a few moments. She kissed me on the cheek and walked out of the clinic with a broad smile on her face. I smiled even more then. After all, she called me, "young man."

A lesson from Anonymous, our wise teacher, always helps: "I never lie about my age. I tell people I'm my wife's age and then lie about hers."

I once went to a nightclub in Manhattan to hear some young comics. A female comic appearing that evening spotted me in the audience and declared to everyone in the house, "We've got an old guy here tonight!"

"Old guy?!" I screamed, jumping up on the stage. "I'll show you an old guy!" I grabbed her firmly and danced her wildly around the stage, and hugged her as the audience went mad.

An elderly woman of seventy-five was told by her doctor that she was pregnant. She immediately found a phone to call her seventy-three year old husband, to tell him of this incredible news.

"You old son-of-a gun," she exclaimed. "You made me pregnant. I'm going to have your baby!"

"Who is this?" was the old geezer's reply.

Anonymous: "Inside every older person is a younger person wondering what the hell happened." As you can see, I do appreciate his wisdom.

One of the positive things about getting older is that we don't need to drink alcohol any more. We only need to just stand up fast to get the same effect.

Just think: I'm older than the President of the United States and the next Prime Minister of Israel. I also get up a lot more at night to go to the toilet. Getting up at six in the morning is seriously over-sleeping for me. Yogi Berra once declared, "I get up at six every morning no matter what time it is."

I'm optimistic. Not everyone gets to see the sunrise every morning. I have noticed that as my age goes up, everything else seems to come down. I walk into a room more than ten times a day asking myself, "What did I want to do here?" The only trouble with getting old is that there is no future in it.

A man walked up to his house and noticed his grandfather sitting half-naked on the front porch.

"Grandfather, what are you doing sitting out here without your pants on?"

The old man slowly looked at his grandson and replied, "Well, last week I sat out here with no shirt on and got a stiff neck. Your grandmother sent me out here with no pants on. It's her idea."

I also notice gray hair in places I hadn't seen before. Now that I'm sixty-four, my wife can finally relax and believe I'm faithful. Actually, if I had known I was going to live this long, I'd have taken better care of myself. I keep thinking, "I'm too young to be this old."

At this age, something terrible happens to music. How I loved the Beatles, Deep Purple, and Pink Floyd. Now all of a sudden it seems like noise. Even worse, I get on an elevator and hear them only as background music.

Getting older is all about high blood pressure, high cholesterol, high anxiety, and low sex drive. At my age, "safe sex" is not falling out of bed.

My compact disc changer is loaded with music of the Fifties. When I was fifty, I lived in the Sixties. Now that I'm over sixty, I live in the Fifties.

Sophie Tucker (a very famous saloon singer/comedienne from the 1930's to the early 1960's) once suggested: "From birth to age eighteen, a girl needs good parents. From eighteen to thirty-five, she needs good looks. From thirty-five to fifty-five, she needs a good personality. And from fifty-five on, she needs cash."

I suddenly realized that when Shakespeare was my age, he was already dead for 22 years! Getting older, I realize that everything that doesn't hurt doesn't work.

Marick Chazin, a good friend of mine and a fellow Gestalt psychotherapist, told me that he sees me as actually getting younger every day because of my new life style of traveling, teaching, learning, performing, and doing workshops. He said that he also noticed that I'm in love with life, and that I live every moment in the here and now, love being with people, loving them and sharing my "child-within" with them.

He has noticed that when I share my "child" with others, it brings them to a place where they can share their "child" with mc, which allows an encounter of two children meeting in adult bodies. This is constant happiness to Mark Chazin. Even sadness becomes happiness when two children in adult bodies share and play with the pain.

"By living like this. you get younger and younger," Marick related to me.

Bob Dylan sings: "I was an old man once. I'm much younger now."

As I was going for my morning walk a while back, I noticed a senior citizen walking on a pair of crutches that had wheels. I stopped him and asked him about his crutches. He showed me that he also had a set of brakes controlled by handgrips.

"Can you dance with this thing?" I asked, astonished.

He looked up at me with a sparkle in his eyes.

"Only the Boogie Woogie," he smiled.

A baby first communicates with his environment through smiles, chuckles, and laughter. "It's great to be alive," relates the baby through her giggles. The rest is given through confirmation by her parents. Her caregivers let the child know, all through her young life, that laughter is permissible, and that she has the right to be here on this earth. The child learns that she is allowed to live life as play and have fun, and that humor and laughter are absolutely essential for survival.

Except if you're Jewish. If you are Jewish, you were then born to suffer. "Life sucks and then you get to die!"

Jewish foreplay, by the way, is two hours of begging. Then there is Jewish sexual compatibility, which is when they both have a headache on the same night.

When my children were growing up, and even to this day, there was and still is laughter in the air, even through the painful moments. We mostly always related to each other speaking in English or Italian accents, or talking on the phone like the Mafia, or with Southern American mountain accents.

When my sons were drafted into the army, I told them to take their sense of humor with them. It would lift their morale and the morale of the others in their unit.

By the way, you can never win in raising children. My second son came to me one day and complained, "Dad, you really screwed me up."

"How?" I asked cautiously.

"You gave me too much love. If you had just been a little tough on me, I might have been more today than I am. But, no, you had to accept me and love me as I am!"

See? You can't win. If it's not one thing, it's another.

Two drug addict parents watch as their child goes off to college and wonder to one another, "Where did we go right?"

When I was on the operating table undergoing my angioplasty, the doctor told me that I would have to sign a consent statement in order for him to insert a tiny balloon in me to clear the passage to my heart.

"What am I signing?" I asked, seeking more clarification.

"In case things don't go so well," he began to explain once again, "and we might have to perform open-heart surgery," he continued, tilting the consent form so that I could see it and sign it. "Are you ready to sign?"

"Oh, that's great!" I joked, raising my voice a bit. "I came here for a simple angioplasty and I'm ending up with open heart surgery!"

"Maybe you want your wife to sign?" another doctor then implied graciously.

"Oh, sure.!" I laughed drolly. "And if anything happens to me, she'll have to carry the guilt with her all her life? No thanks. I don't dislike her that much."

I signed. And guess what? I'm still here.

My three children came to visit me in the hospital. To cheer me up, they brought me comic books and funny audiotapes. Now, try to imagine the hospital machine that monitors our heart beat. It goes "Blip!" and the line arcs up, then slopes down. Then there is another "Blip!" and on the screen the line goes up and down again, right within eyesight from my bed.

Well, there we all were, my children and I, when all of a sudden we failed to see the line go up and down—the arc indicating that I was still alive had stopped blipping.

"Ahhhhh!!!" I screamed—so loudly that the machine started up again by itself! It was as if my scream had mimicked a kind of heartbeat that jumped-started the monitor I was hooked up to. Talk about miracle of miracles!

It was hysterical to all of us.

When I read *Time Magazine*, I scan the obituary column to see if there is anyone who has died who was younger than I am. I read to see if they drank alcohol or smoked or ate fatty foods, or whatever life style they had lived. According to the genes I inherited from my parents, I am, as of today, enjoying ten extra years that they didn't. My father passed away at the age of fifty-four.

When my father died, I was relieved. He had suffered from Huntington's Chorea, which attacks the nervous system and leaves the victim a jumbling, mumbling sack of ticks, with impeded speech and a loss of bodily control. For a teenager, that was a catastrophe. How could I bring friends home and introduce them to my father?

I was sad when he died, and joyful. A load was lifted from my shoulders. He was a man full of mirth, smiles, and rage. He was the one who taught me how to make peroxide when I was seven years old.

"You take a little peroxide and mix it with more peroxide, and—wham!— you've got peroxide!" he instructed me often.

That was a lovely first joke to a young kid.

It was even lovelier to have come from my father.

Medical researchers have concluded that the first five minutes of life are the most dangerous and critical. They have also discovered that the last five minutes of life are not so hot either.

When the Pope visited Israel in March of 2000, an eighty-year-old man approached the Holy Father and requested that the Pope grant him a few moments of his time.

"Holy Father, I'm 80 years old and last night I had sex with two eighteen-year-old girls, twice in one night," he said excitedly.

"How long has it been since your last confession?" the Pope inquired of the old gentleman solemnly.

"Never!" corrected the old man, bemused. "I'm Jewish."

"So why are you telling me all this?" the Pope questioned, startled. *"Telling you? I'm telling everyone!"* snapped the old geezer.

Having sex when you get to be my age is still wonderful. It just gets more and more difficult to see with whom you're having it. It seems that after the age of fifty, I began to age at the rate of about three years per year. I began falling asleep fifteen minutes into an episode of Seinfeld. I also began falling asleep during sex rather than after.

Groucho Marx once said, "Anyone can get old. All you have to do is live long enough."

Death is the greatest experience of all. That's why it's saved for last.

How about when I look for my glasses only to find them on my forehead? The future isn't what it used to be.

I worry about gaining weight. The only time I can see my putz now is when I look in the mirror. And when I look in the mirror, I think, "When did all this happen?"

When I'm at the beach, I work like a mule to keep my gut sucked in. After the girls walk by, I can then let my stomach out with a sigh of relief.

Muhammad Ali said, "If people view the world at fifty as they did at twenty, they have wasted thirty years of their lives."

Hector Berlioz said," Time is a great teacher. Unfortunately, it kills all its pupils."

Yes, I've witnessed people crying over the fact that youth has passed them by, and that things are not the same as they used to be. The toughest thing about growing old is remembering our youth. Well, I have news for you. Things are never supposed to be as they were before. The only thing constant is change.

High up at the topmost part of a palm tree, the leaves are sprouting green. The palm tree is not interested in the brown, dead parts that have fallen away. The green parts keep renewing themselves, and the tree lets the dead parts be the memories of what once was.

Isn't that us, too? We are, sort of like the palm tree, to go forward, remembering who we were, and loving who we are. Can you imagine a butterfly mourning over the fact that she is no longer a cocoon?

"Where are the good old days?" some people cry.

There's a lyric that croons, "I'd sell all my tomorrows for just one yesterday." Yes, I, too, could fantasize how great things used to be, and walk around with a cloud over my head and let it rain only on me. Or I could concentrate on making today the memories of tomorrow.

"Just think. I'm ten years younger now than I will be ten years from now," Anonymous has pointed out to us on several occasions.

"You know you're getting older when you've got money to burn, but the fire has gone out," he (she?) has suggested at other times.

Anonymous is the one who never seems to grow older!

Suddenly we realize that life is a terminal disease and the world will still spin merrily around after we are gone. For people who don't want to believe that this lovely celebration called Life will one-day end, let me tell them this. Researchers have discovered, after checking out names of people who were born two hundred years ago, that, statistically speaking, 100% of the people who were born have died. So, given this bit of news, what do you imagine our chances are?

These researchers have also discovered the cause of death: *Life*. So it's not a question of if we take the trip from the womb to the tomb. We will. The question is, however, a question of how will we? Some people call this the journey of from Viagra to Niagara. Or how about—from sperm to worm?

A young man planned to spend that evening at home with two young beauties; so he asked his doctor to write him a prescription for Viagra. Upon arriving home, the man proceeded in swallowing the entire bottle of pills in preparation for the event. The next day he arrived at the doctor's office looking as if a truck had run over him.

"What happened?" the doctor inquired.

"They never showed up!" cried the man. So the doctor put his hand in a cast and sent him home.

"We do all we can to live longer," Anonymous reminds us. "We eat healthy, exercise often, and die anyway. I gave up the beer but kept the belly."

In optimism and humor is how I live this moment. Do I want more than I have or do I decide to be happy with who I am and what I have at this very moment? In Pirkei Avot, the Sages teach: "Who is rich? The one who is happy with what he has." A Sage always answers his own question.

Anonymous must be a Sage. "At twenty," he confesses, "I didn't care what the world thought of me. At thirty, I began to worry what the world thought of me. At fifty, I discovered that the world wasn't thinking of me at all."

There are changes going on all the time. I can't go back to what I once was; so I try to fall in love with the changes and with who I am now. Why shouldn't happiness be something to experience all the time rather than something to try to recall all the time?

Okay, so my pants keep creeping up on me. By the age of sixty-four, I became a pair of pants and a head. My pants have come all the way up to my armpits. So what? I love waking up in the morning in pain. How else would I know that I was still alive? And now it takes me a full hour in the morning just to get ready to drink my coffee, which lately tastes like dish water. So what? I have a list of fifty things I want to do before I die and have only done two of them. So what? Isn't life grand? Like, what's the alternative?

I knew it was difficult to adapt to change some years ago when I was first unable to find a simple typewriter in an office full of computers. I didn't make my first million at thirty, and at sixty-four things are not looking to improve very much. I still wake up at three in the morning regretting the dumb decisions I made at twenty. Then I realize that it's all part of the journey I had to take in order to get where I am today. It's all grist for the mill and in a hundred years from now, who the hell will know the difference anyway?

I walked into a restaurant with some friends of mine once.

"What would you like?" The hostess asked politely.

Being the sprite show-off that I am, I smiled broadly a bit.

"I'd like a pretty girl of about 22 years old, if you've got one?" I requested. The customer is always right, after all.

"Do you want her for adoption?" was her quick, cutting reply.

An elderly man was walking down the street when suddenly a frog leaped in his path.

"Kiss me!" pleaded the frog. "Kiss me! I'm a lovely princess and will do anything your heart desires for the rest of your life."

The man bent down, picked the frog up, put her in his pocket, and continued on his way. After some time, the anxious frog peeped her head out from the man's pocket and cajoled, "Why don't you kiss me so that I can turn into a lovely princess and become your slave?"

The man extracted the frog from his pocket.

"At my age, dear princess," he informed her calmly, "a talking frog will do."

Sex can be hilarious at my age. A colleague of mine (approximately my age) decided to buy some edible panties for his wife to wear. Hoping to eat them off her right away, he rushed home and gave them to her. She was thrilled; so much so that her joy became contagious as the two of them, while trying to remain cool, laughed hysterically as they tried to figure out what part of the panties he should start eating first.

They ended up laughing so hard that tears flowed down their cheeks. By the way, after my friend told me this story about their adventure, I didn't ask them if they ever wound up having sex. If they didn't, I'm sure that my friend at least didn't walk away hungry. I wonder what flavor the panties were?

I've discovered that by getting older, my wife and I don't fight anymore. We laugh about things more now. George Burns once quipped: "When I bend down to pick something up, I take some extra time to look around to see if there is anything else I can do before deciding to come back up."

I keep feeling that I have a great future behind me. I have become cognizant of the fact that everything I learned in school has been obsolete for the past thirty years, and that I need the help of a teen-ager to load my computer for me.

I went to my fortieth high school reunion in 1995. What a mistake! I suggest you never do this, unless you want to see a bunch of old men and women running around talking about their surgical operations and about how successfully their grandchildren married. The kid who always wanted to be a lawyer is now retired and plays golf most of the time, while his kid is a lawyer fulltime.

And—wouldn't you know it?-all they remember is how stupid I was and the goof-offs I pulled in high school.

"Remember the time they pulled you in for under-aged drinking, Ravich?"

I still have a soft spot for the "old gang." The fact is, they are really the old gang now. What I witnessed at this reunion was how really fast these super sonic years have flipped by. That chick in high school—the one I couldn't stop thinking about in my youth—is now that old lady with the incredibly fat nose, slumped over there in the corner. They all looked so old, and I don't understand why they had such a hard time recognizing me.

An elderly man watches as a teenager, with orange and purple hair and earrings all over his body, walks by.

"What are you staring at? Haven't you ever done anything daring in your life, old man?" snarls the boy.

"Yes, I have," answered the bemused elderly gentleman." I once had sex with a parrot and thought that you might be my son."

I guess wisdom does come with age.

I plan to keep working, studying, and growing. What about you? Will you dance life or drag it? Getting older is an honor. It's just that I would like to honor someone else with it.

CHAPTER TEN

Education and the Absurd

The greatest thing I have ever done in my life was to be present when someone needed me.

—Bernie Segal

Humor and education: this phrase sounds like an oxymoron, doesn't it? We all know that kids are attracted to humorous adults. Humor displays our human side and brings us closer to people. Victor Borge, the recently deceased pianist/comedian, once suggested, "A smile is the shortest distance between two people."

I'd like to change Borge's aphorism to: "A smile from a teacher is the shortest distance to the pupil."

"When I laugh with my pupils," Rachel, an English teacher in Israel, and a very close friend of mine, said to me once, "it is an act of love. By sharing smiles and laughter, I show my love and concern. They feel it and respond in kind."

"I love my profession," Limor, a Bible teacher, once told me. "I respect my pupils and this respect becomes a two-way street. The influence we have on each other is mutual. I create the student and he/she creates me at the same time. Without this mutual impact, there is no connection. I must have this connection and I get it a lot through humor."

And yet, in many cases, school may be the last place where one finds humor, creativity, smiles and humanity. I know. There are the exceptions and there are very human educators. You went to school. How many can you count?

I will always remember my first grade teacher, Ms. Chase. It was such a pleasure and so great a feeling of safety to be near a woman who had accepted me unconditionally. She made sure that she had lunched in the home of every one of her pupils. When I was ill, she took the class to the library, where there was a phone, and made sure every classmate wished me well. Her concern for our little souls has had an effect on me till this very day.

Unfortunately, on the whole, there is not enough of this kind of empathy, or, for that matter, humor either, in academia today. On the other hand, I can understand. Academia is serious stuff, serious business, after all: dead serious, in fact. Grades and content sometimes appear more important than the children. The teacher has to complete the material before the end of the year. Kids only interfere with this.

Very few people know what a teacher is faced with on a daily basis: an unmotivated student or two, angry parents, critical principals, and dissatisfied supervisors. The tension remains long after the school day ends. The emotional pain and drainage are excruciating. The best way for a teacher to deal with inevitable burnout is to discern the humor in human affairs—and to start laughing as soon as possible. This sense of discernment could very well save a teacher's life.

I agree completely with Joel Goodman's definition of a teacher: "A person who can drink two cups of coffee at 7:00 in the morning and hold on to it until 2:00 in the afternoon."

My first encounter with the Israeli school system came when I, a high school English teacher, was asked to monitor a Hebrew grammar matriculation exam at the end of the school year. The reasoning for this was because I then possessed only a slight knowledge of the Hebrew language (I later became totally fluent.), and I would not be tempted to take pity on the students during the "holy of holies"—exam week, that is—and help them.

I watched, in a state of disbelief, as the students cheated without making any effort to hide it from me.

"Students! I'm being paid by the Board of Education," I, outraged and startled, admonished, "to make sure you don't cheat! Please honor the contract."

This warning only forced them to become subtler and more creative in their manner of cheating, so as not to offend me. Just when I, even more frustrated now, began to comment on the fact that they were continuing to cheat, only more creatively, the homeroom teacher burst into the room.

"I heard you are not letting them cheat!" he screeched. "Why don't you let them cheat? What do you care?"

At first, I was stunned, but later discovered that a teacher's professional standing rested on the results of what his/her students get on the matriculation examination. I was supposed to supervise the exam, but God forbid if I wouldn't allow them to cheat. And for this I was being paid!

Before intense exam days, kids cram for such exams, sweat all the time, and get diarrhea, only to vomit the material out on the day of the exam. And then two days after the test, they forget 85% of what they had learned.

When my eldest son showed me his report card from high school with all A's, I frowned my disapproval. "What are you, some kind of a clerk?" I asked sarcastically. He later consulted with me before going on to professional acting school. "Learn as much as you can," I advised him, "and forget it as fast as possible." He has become a successful actor today.

When I used humor to encapsulate a lesson I was teaching, I noticed, the material itself became more digestible to the students. I remember once looking out over my classroom during a lesson, when I spotted a student I had never seen before, taking notes.

"What are you doing here?" I insisted to him. "You don't belong in my class, do you?"

"Please let me sit here and listen to you," he pleaded. "My English teacher threw me out of her lesson for disturbing her, and I love being here." Needless to say, I let him stay. The kid was hungry for humor, and also for some joy in his learning time.

One mother once furiously burst into my class during my lesson and demanded that her son come home with her immediately.

"He's got a high fever," she apologetically murmured, "but didn't want to miss your lesson." Only when they left together did I notice the boy's pajamas tucked neatly under his jeans.

Every year I would begin my first lesson by ceremoniously announcing, "Boys and girls, I came into this world to have fun. I plan to do just that this year. If, while we're having fun, you choose to learn English, be my guest. The moment I stop having fun, I'm out of here."

I turned my lessons into Abbott and Costello routines, such as the skit fans refer to as "Who's on First?"

In Hebrew, English 'who' is Hebrew *he*.

English 'he' in Hebrew is *she*.

While English 'she' translated into Hebrew yields he.

All of which brings us back to English 'she', which is Hebrew he, which actually, in Hebrew, sounds like English 'who'.

I'm sure that some learning took place each time I chanted these pronouns for the first time to students, since even the weakest pupils left the lesson reciting, "'Who' is 'he' and 'she' is 'he' and. . . ."—smiling and laughing all the while.

Humor opens the body's pores so that information may be completely absorbed.

I have observed that humor and play can restore a sense of proportion, make problems of learning less threatening, and therefore reduce our resistance to learning new concepts that might normally appear so threatening as to overwhelm us. We overcome our problems the moment we learn to laugh at them.

If teachers truly love their pupils, the results are amazing. Love and loyalty are returned. Super human feats are demonstrated when mutual respect is shown. Children need charismatic adults who show caring and build bridges of empathy. Empathy is putting oneself in the shoes of the other.

"What is this pupil feeling, thinking? How can I meet his/her needs?" are questions all teachers should constantly ask themselves. Trying to meet the needs of over thirty pupils who are totally and uniquely different one from the other can be exhausting.

I regret having to say this, but I would actually begin to hate those pupils whose needs were too impossible to fulfill.

As in most schools in Israel, each semester brings the homeroom teacher together with the individual subject matter teacher to discuss the grades of each pupil before they are written into "The Book of Life."

"Okay, let's talk about Avi," suggested the homeroom teacher. "What did he get in History?"

The History teacher announced, "Four"(Out of ten).

"What about his math?"

"Five" reported the math teacher, and so on—till they got to me.

"What does he get in English?" she asked.

"Nine," I reported.

There was silence.

The teachers began to move around uncomfortably.

How could the dummy Avi possibly get a nine in English? He never did his homework, they stammered. In their classes, this was perhaps true.

This same scenario was repeated for Haya, Sara, Mordichai, etc. The scene resembled a ping-pong game, what with their necks snapping towards my direction at every grade that was reported by me at 3 or 4 points higher than they had ever conceived imaginable for this or that student! But it was no hoax. I was doing something just not ever done before in Israel!

These kids were fantastic with me. They well deserved the grades that I had given them. They had worked hard, had shown interest and motivation. How? By my showing them respect, of course—for where they were, and not where they should be. By my treating every kid as if he/she were a "little professor."

I like to think of myself as being very much in touch with other people and with what they are feeling. Apropos of that, when I sensed that the students in my classes were bored, I would shift directions.

"Okay. You don't want to learn my way," I would observe. "So how do you want to learn this stuff?"

I discovered that some classes loved singing the latest popular hits they heard on the radio and from MTV. I struggled. I researched and learned these songs well enough to present them to the class and began teaching them. I taught them to sing what they had so wanted to learn. Their attitude changed completely. What fun! Singing to learn English!

One class in particular begged me to play ping-pong with them, instead of having the usual lesson. I promised them that we could on one condition.

"We play in English. No speaking Hebrew. Agreed?"

They agreed, but I was overwhelmed when they began swearing at missed balls, turning to me for the translation of "Oh, shit!" or "Screw you!" I had to do it. I had promised.

But I had no idea that I was causing waves of gossip elsewhere, until the school principal asked to see me.

"I understand that your pupils are receiving high grades," he said sternly.

"Yes," I blurted proudly, sensing that he was sincerely preparing the moment to give me a compliment.

"A good teacher fails his pupils," he retorted seriously.

I was traumatized.

"But I'm being paid to help them succeed, not fail," I innocently responded.

"You're too easy. A good teacher fails his pupils," he repeated, more sternly now.

I began to wonder if I could fit into a system that treated failure as success.

Just before the Jewish New Year each year, the principal usually invites all of his 100 plus teachers to drink a toast to the new beginnings. He personally gave each of us a plastic soap dish as a gift for this occasion. I thought kindly of a man who would give me a plastic soap dish as a gift.

When I returned to my classroom after the holidays, I was bewildered by the lack of not even one tiny piece of chalk in the classrooms; a teaching tool that had always been present in abundance before.

I rushed to the office to ask the secretary to give me some chalk.

"Where is your plastic soap dish?" she inquired.

"At home with the soap," I responded with surprise. "Why?"

"I'm not allowed to give you chalk without your soap dish," she admonished. She remained adamant. I was taken aback.

"What does a soap dish have to do with chalk?" I asked in frustration.

"No soap dish, no chalk," she repeated officiously. I returned to my lesson and apologized to my pupils for not having chalk and continued the lesson anyway.

At the closing bell of the lesson, the principal showed up.

"I heard that you asked for chalk without your soap dish," he exclaimed. "Well, let me show you something." He took a piece of chalk from a soap dish he was holding, threw in on the floor, and stepped on it, smashing it with his shoe.

"You see that?" He then looked at me in silence. I thought that this was some sort of Israeli ritual, the sort we see in the movies, where the young Yugoslav soldier slugs down a cognac and dashes the cognac glass into the fireplace.

So, not to be impolite, I took a piece of chalk myself, threw it on the floor and smashed it with my shoe and said, "You see that?" I hoped that I was complying properly with the "Israeli Chalk Smashing Ceremony."

I next expected him to dance around the smashed chalk with some ritual chanting.

"Now do you understand why I asked you to bring your plastic soap dish? If you don't put the chalk away in the soap dish after each lesson, the floor could become messy," he said self-righteously.

It slowly began to dawn on me exactly the kind of people I was dealing with: strange ones!

Oh, well, nobody's perfect.

A teacher tries to demonstrate the dangers of alcoholism to her pupils by dropping a worm into a glass of whiskey. The worm immediately gives up the ghost and the teacher asks, "What do we learn from this?"

"If you drink whiskey, you'll never have worms!" one student shouted out.

At the end of each school year, Mr. Soap Dish (aka, the Principal) held a mandatory meeting with all of the teachers on his staff. To this very day, I still can't figure out why Mr. Soap Dish thought it important to inform the large gathering of teachers that the "final grades that were given by the individual subject matter teachers failed to match the grades given by the examiners hired by the Board of Education." He cited English, the subject that I teach, as a case in point. His insinuation meant that I had been padding the grades, which, according to him, were way off the mark.

With all the other teachers present to bear witness, I asked the principal to read the grades aloud, knowing full well that my grades had matched the Board's almost perfectly. I had been a supervisor at the same period that I had been teaching and was professionally trained and experienced in the proper appreciation of scores.

"Mr. Ravich," he politely announced, "I can't take the time from this meeting, but the grades are in my office and you can discuss them with me later." This was no less than public humiliation, indicating that I was cheating. I was sorely confused.

I patiently waited for the end of his lecture, and proceeded to walk with him to his office. He fumbled around with the drawers of his desk, pretending to look for the grades.

He mumbled, "I can't seem to find them. Perhaps you should come back in the morning."

I then placed my chair against the door and sat down in it.

"No one's going home until you find those scores," I smiled.

I've discovered that smiling takes the sting out of the rage.

He accused me of being silly, but when he realized that I had no intention of budging from my place at the door, he began looking for the grades once again. Finally, as if by a miracle, he found them. I carefully read them over, and just as I had expected, my grades were completely in line with those given by the Board of Education.

When I questioned him about this, he quickly apologized.

"I've been confusing you, Mr. Ravich, with the math teacher and her scores. Isn't that terrible?" Going further, he attempted to sidetrack the subject.

"How am I supposed to react when the math scores don't match up with the Board's?" He almost had me.

But then, I began to laugh out loud and proceeded to give him my chimpanzee number: crouching to the floor, putting one hand on my stomach, the other on the top of my head, scratching myself, and making "Cheetah" sounds with my tongue rolled over my upper teeth.

I teach this method as a way of relieving stress.

At the close of the school year, I advised the principal that he'd best start looking for another teacher to take my place, because I was preparing my resignation. The principal looked at me with a shocked expression.

"You're leaving education? What will you do instead?" I thought hard for a moment before answering.

"Well, the worst thing that could happen is that I'll become homeless. On second thought, I prefer that to working here."

When faced with tough decisions, I always ask myself, *What's the worst thing that could happen if I choose 'X' over 'Y'?* When I do this, the catastrophic fantasy doesn't seem so bad, after all. I must stay true to my heart if health, physical and mental, is to be my top priority.

The researchers for the best selling *Chicken Soup for the Soul* tell of an experience of the early 1960s, in a predominantly black Harlem, New York, elementary school, about a staff of young social workers who volunteered to study the cases of the school's students. At the end of the school year, they reported that in most cases, a large majority of the pupils wouldn't stand a chance at succeeding to achieve the American Dream, since some had come from broken homes, and others from backgrounds of drugs and prostitution.

Thirty years past, and these same social workers returned to check whether their predictions had indeed been borne out. They were amazed to discover that the subjects of their study had not only succeeded but had surpassed anyone's wildest expectations. They had become high ranking officers in the armed forces, bank managers, teachers, etc.

When each one was asked how he/she had managed to succeed so well, they all gave the same answer: "Mrs. Johnson was responsible for my success." These same social workers decided to look for Ms. Johnson and learn of her secret.

After an extensive search, Mrs. Johnson was finally found in an old folks' home. They requested a meeting with her. She shuttled in on two canes and stared at the social workers.

"We asked the children you had taught how they had managed to succeed so well and how they had found such happiness in their lives. They all said, 'Mrs. Johnson was responsible for my success.'"

"What is your secret?" a member of the staff asked of Mrs. Johnson.

Mrs. Johnson sat silently for a moment and then innocently whispered, "I just loved them."

As I now write *A Funny Thing Happened on the Way to Enlightenment*, I am the director of the Gestalt Institute of Tel Aviv. Most people don't know what Gestalt is. It has to do with teaching people to communicate through their present experience. When people ask me what the difference between Gestalt and psychoanalysis is, I relate the following tale to illustrate:

> *"There was once a man who stuttered. He decided at some point in his life to go to psychoanalysis for a cure.*
>
> *After a year on the couch, his wife asked him how therapy was working.*
>
> *"I s-s-still s-s-stutter, but now I understand w-w-why," he replied.*
>
> *He then decided to seek something more experiential at the Gestalt Institute. After one year had passed, his wife asked*

the same question: "How is Gestalt helping?"

"I s-s-still s-s-stutter, but now I e-e-experience it," he stammered.

He finally went to a workshop called, "Short term Therapy. "This is a "quickie" workshop, in which, at the conclusion, all the participants return home in order to get divorced. But they hug first. Upon returning home from this workshop, his wife approached him again.

"Did the workshop help?" she ask hopefully.

"Peter Piper picked a peck of pickled peppers," he began to utter. "If Peter Piper picked a peck of pickled peppers, where are the pickled peppers Peter Piper picked?"

"Why, that's wonderful!" exclaimed his wife.

"Yeah, "he stammered, "b-b-but who in the hell w-w-wants t-t-to keep saying t-t-that all day?!"

During their sabbaticals from school, scores of Israeli schoolteachers attend my institute and take a course I call The Human Dialogue. I started this course in 1988 and until this day, the Board of Education does not allow me to give grades to teachers, which would entitle them to get an automatic raise in their salaries. This dictate came from the Teacher Training Department.

"How can you give a grade when your course is experiential?" they questioned. "It's not academic. Therefore, it's not serious enough. We want our instructors to know the subject they teach more in depth. We don't need our teachers wasting their time on trivia."

What they really meant is: "We don't want teachers losing time learning to be human."

I am not surprised. The Teacher Training Department of the Board of Education still believes that by intensifying the knowledge of the subject, teachers will naturally produce successful learners. All the knowledge in the world will not help a teacher make contact with a child. The one most important element in teaching is making contact, and for the Board of Education that's not kosher.

The easiest thing for teachers to do is to give each child a "downer" pill before the lesson; the result would be that all of the youngsters would end up staring at their shoes. For the Board of Education, that would be great, since now the teacher can, at last, complete the material before the end of the semester.

"If there are three birds on a limb," a math teacher asked her fifth grade class, "and Billy shoots one bird, how many birds remain?" Danny knew he had the answer.

"Teacher, if Billy shoots one of the birds, all of them will fly away because of the noise."

"That's true, Danny, but for this exercise the answer is two. Two birds will be left. But I like your line of thinking."

The next day Danny came in with a picture.

"Teacher, there are three women eating ice cream cones in this picture. One is licking the ice cream, one is staring at it and smiling, and one is sucking it. In your opinion, which one is married?"

"I think it's the one who is sucking the ice cream," answers the teacher knowingly.

"No," corrects Danny, "it's the one with the wedding ring. But I like your line of thinking."

At my Gestalt Institute, some teachers on sabbatical leave become depressed after the Passover Holidays.

"Why the depression?" I ask.

"The sabbatical year is almost over and we have to return to school soon." The answer from these devoted educators is invariably the same. This can only mean that school is the one place in the world where teachers and pupils have something in common. They both hate to be there. School becomes the holy meeting place where all those concerned can share fear, depression, rage, and shame.

"Why is there violence in schools?" we then ask.

Imagine the following story: A mother comes to her son's room in the morning.

"Benny, get up. It's seven o'clock and you'll be late for school."

Benny turns over and goes back to sleep crying, "I'm not going to school. I hate school."

"But you have to go to school," his mother pleads.

"There are over a hundred teachers who despise me and over a thousand students that can't bear the sight of me. Give me one good reason why I should go to school?"

His mother leans over to him. "I'll give you two reasons, not one," she whispers softly. "First of all, you're forty-five years old. And secondly, you're the principal of the school."

Instead of being a place of warmth, love, patience, understanding, and respect, schools have become the hot bed, except for a few cases, of blame, humiliation, shame, anger, and fear. I believe the teacher's credo should be, as Sam Horn suggests in *Conzentration*: "We are here to serve, not to shine. We are here to give good, not to look good. We are here to make a difference, not to make a name."

Some school supervisors, superintendents, and principals use their position of power to shame and disgrace teachers. It's no wonder that this is sometimes passed on into the classroom.

Now, if I may, I would like to offer a few words about shame and humiliation. When someone is shamed, he dies a little. Why else do you think people refer to death when they say, "I was *dying* of shame." Or: "I was so embarrassed, I wanted to bury myself. I wanted the earth to *swallow* me up!" Or we might hear someone exclaim, "If I'm called on to volunteer to speak, over my *dead* body will I make a fool out of myself in front of all those people!"

There's a lot of death taking place in some schools.

As a supervisor, I disliked firing teachers, but sometimes I had no other choice. When educators are recommended for dismissal, the teacher's union defends them by attempting to get them back into the system. I would always agree to their arguments, on one condition. I would allow the teacher to go back, if those who were defending the teacher would give me the names of their children and where they go to school. Then they must agree that this same instructor come to their children's school to be their child's teacher. Silence usually follows such a suggestion.

As school supervisor, I was responsible for bringing many children into The State of Israel. Whenever I submitted a dismissal notice to a teacher, she would immediately become pregnant. The union does not allow the firing of a pregnant teacher. I sincerely lost count as to how many children were born as a result of this threat.

While I was a supervisor of English Instruction, I received the following letter from a teacher under my supervision: "Knowing you has been of no advantage to me. You have been a great disappointment in my professional career."

My first reaction was to single this teacher out for revenge. But then I thought, "This letter is her truth. Why should my wall be papered with documents, certificates of my successes and letters of appreciation only? Where is my honesty if I fail to show my 'dark side'?" So I had her letter framed and put on the wall of my office at the Board of Education. Whenever anyone came to my office seeking my professional advice, I would guide them to where the letter was hung, point and say, "Know thee before whom ye stand."

As a teacher, I refrained from giving grades, since, among other things, I believe that giving grades provokes the market mentality in students. Arguments would ensue concerning the grades. Parents would call my home, and I disliked this kind of a relationship with people. Instead, I requested that the pupils grade themselves. Who knows better than the pupils themselves how much they have improved, how much motivation they have in doing projects, etc?

The surprise was that when pupils grade themselves, they usually rate themselves lower than I would have. I spent most of my energy trying to convince them to raise their grade rather than lower it. My insistence became the market in reverse. They created the weekly exam, with my supervision, and a special crew would grade the exam. I also requested that they grade me with suggestions on how to improve myself, without their having to sign their names. This gave me an indication of what was missing in my style of making contact with them.

I do not ever, in all my years as a teacher and supervisor, remember training courses or workshops for educators in which the emphasis was on making contact, creating empathy, or in becoming a more loving, humorous, and generous human being. Most of the training courses that I had attended were concerned with the teacher's subject matter, understanding the material, and becoming familiar with new concepts and curriculum that, in my opinion, were designed to confuse just about everybody.

Whenever I need to lighten myself up, I remind myself of the prayer from AA meetings: "Dear God, give me the strength to change what I can change, the courage to accept what I cannot change, and the wisdom to know the difference between the two." I would like to add, "And bless me with a sense of humor and an ability to laugh at the absurdity of it all."

Instead of meeting children where they are, some teachers complain that the pupils are not where they should be. They blame the teacher who taught them previously for being incompetent. "If their last teacher had taught properly, these students would have known the material!" is the cry heard every year from the disgruntled educator. Little do they realize that next year's teacher will be saying the same thing about them!

Some pupils are reminded of how they're not okay. Some teachers call or write home to the parents to tell them how not okay their kids are, and then there is tension in the home, and private teachers are sought afterward by the parents. I could never understand how a system could call itself successful, when a large part of the population must hire private teachers to teach the children what the public school should have taught them in the first place. I personally have heard teachers telling pupils who have struggled to understand the lesson, "Get a private teacher. I don't have time for you. I have to cover the material."

I think it's the system's duty to meet the children where they are and guide them in the direction they are going and growing, rather than to bend them out of shape trying to mold them into the images of what we want them to be or think they ought to be.

To me, educating children, whether at school or at home, is related somehow to a tale I once came across on the Internet. The originator of this tale is unknown to me.

Two men, both seriously ill, occupied the same hospital room. One man was allowed to sit up for one hour each afternoon. His bed was next to the room's only window. The other man had to spend all his time flat on his back. The men talked for hours on end about their families, home, jobs, and hopes. And every afternoon when the man in the bed by the window could sit up, he would pass the time by describing to his roommate all the things he could see through the window.

The man in the other bed began to live for these one-hour periods, where his world would be broadened and enlivened by all the activity and color of the world outside.

His window overlooked a park with a lovely lake. Ducks and swans played on the water while children sailed their model boats. Young lovers walked arm in arm amidst flowers of every color of the rainbow. As the man by the window described it all in exquisite detail, the man on the other side of the room would close his eyes and imagine the picturesque scene.

One day, the nurse came by to bring water for their baths, only to find the lifeless body of the man by the window. He had died peacefully in his sleep. She was saddened and called the hospital attendants to take the body away. As soon as it seemed appropriate, the other man asked if he could be moved next to the window. The nurse made the switch and left him alone.

Slowly, painfully, he propped himself up on one elbow to take his first look at the world outside. Finally, he would have the joy of seeing it all for himself. He looked out of the window. It faced a blank wall.

"What could have compelled my deceased roommate to describe such wonderful things outside the window when there was nothing but a blank wall?" He asked the nurse, puzzled.

"The deceased was blind and couldn't have possibly seen the wall," she informed him, smiling knowingly. "What he saw was in his mind and he just wanted to encourage you."

Many teachers enter their professions with this approach in their hearts: to enrich others, to give hope, and to encourage children. We all certainly need to learn to internalize the enrichment, hope, and encouragement others may offer us, especially when they are offered with joy, smiles, and laughter.

My daughter was dyslexic long before anyone knew what this was or what to do with it. She was constantly humiliated and shamed about being a "dummy." Even her principal insisted that she repeat the third grade. How's that for encouragement?

I stepped in and demanded that she be tested orally. I showed up a few minutes before the test to demonstrate my support for her. I spoke in English to her in front of the principal because she was also fluent in English, and I knew that the principal would understand practically nothing at all.

Why did I do that?

"Dad, guess what?" a child beams excitedly as she arrives home from school one day. "I saved two dollars! I ran after the bus and missed it. I kept trying to catch it, and every time it came to another station, I missed it again and again, until I found myself at home. Isn't that great?" she beams.

"Why didn't you chase a taxi?" the father, becoming quickly angry, shouts. "You could have saved much more!"

There is a saying that's so old, history itself has long forgotten to whom to attribute it: "My best teachers were my students."

Speaking of our students sometimes being our best teachers, in 1967, I was a schoolteacher in Birmingham, Alabama. It was also the beginning of forced integration, as ordered by the U.S. Supreme Court. No longer would Blacks be forced to drink from their own water fountains, eat in For-Blacks-Only restaurants, use toilet facilities designated only for them, or attend separate schools. For the first time in American history, Blacks were free to enroll in formerly White schools at all levels, from elementary schools to universities.

However, despite the Court's ruling, carrying it out was another matter, especially in Birmingham. Although the Jefferson County Board of Education had jurisdiction over all the schools in the Birmingham area, no efforts were made to change what had been the local rule—rather than what had newly become the national law—for the past two hundred years. Schools in Black areas remained Black and White schools remained White. It would take years before integration was actually something we'd all take for granted.

I volunteered, and the Board assigned me, to a teaching position at an all Black school. I was Jewish, white, and a man, and for the Jefferson County Board of Education, that combination was rarer than a white tiger at the zoo, of which there were none. This exalted teaching position paid $5,000 a year—a sum a bit above the poverty level in 1967.

The four years I spent teaching at that school can only be described as marvelous ones. I learned their local slang, including their home and street dialect, as I all the while had lots of fun also directing some of my pupils in plays and musicals, all performed before large audiences. I loved them and what they did. The more I loved them, the more they let their genius unfold.

During the rehearsals for a musical we were to present at the end of the year, one of my lead actors, a sixteen-year-old boy by the name of Erskine, inexplicably walked out without saying a word, never to be seen again. His text was given to another pupil by the name of Prince, who was very happy to receive it.

After the cast had put in two and a half months of relentless work, Erskine showed up out of nowhere to the dress rehearsal, pale and thin. He had been diagnosed with leukemia. Hoping to play his part on the stage before his inevitable end, he had run away from the hospital with the idea of coming back to rejoin the cast.

When the other actors heard of his intention, they became fearful and angry.

"Don't give his part back to him, Mr. Ravich," they angrily insisted. "We've worked hard and rehearsed long hours. He'll ruin the whole play if you let him perform with us."

I had a dilemma. In a way they were right. He could ruin the whole show. On the other hand, he's dying and must do this part as his last great act on this planet.

I made an appointment with my young Rabbi to consult with him on Jewish Law concerning my conflict.

"According to Jewish Law," he stated, "the play is not the thing. The human being is the thing. This child must get his part back and perform, regardless of the consequences."

I returned to rehearsals with a compromise. Erskine, the boy with leukemia, would play Friday, and Prince, the pupil who had rehearsed up until this time, would play the part Saturday night.

The Friday show went fairly well. Erskine was very weak, but the cast helped him and gave him support; so he made it through just fine. The next day, I invited the cast together to rehearse Prince, who was prepared to play the same part. But Prince surprised me. He didn't seem to be functioning at his best. He suddenly became enraged, tore up his script, and stormed out of the rehearsals.

I had no choice. Erskine, much to his satisfaction, would have to play the part again the second night.

Six weeks later, I met Prince at Erskine's funeral. We sat together while volunteers walked up and down the aisles fanning us from the scorching heat, because air conditioning was unheard of in Black churches at that time.

Amidst the crying, singing and moaning of Erskine's family, Prince approached me, somewhat reluctantly, his voice soft and sincere.

"Mr. Ravich, please don't be mad at me for walking out of rehearsals.

I wasn't really angry. I just played that I was crazy because I wanted Erskine to think that no one else could play the role but him. Do you forgive me?"

No, Prince. I don't forgive you. I admire you. You are my Rabbi.

CHAPTER ELEVEN

I'm Not Leaving Till I Get A Hug

Failure can occur when talent and desire are present in abundance, but optimism is missing.

—Martin E.P. Seligman

I believe that seeing the humor in most situations can get us through the grief and make us feel a lot better. But there are times when humor is not suitable. It can actually cause us grief.

For example, one cold, rainy winter night, the kind of a night when I can think of nothing but the bed, I was awakened by a loud knock at the door. Groggily, I opened it to see a soldier drenched to the skin standing in the doorway.

"You are hereby commanded to report for reserve duty. You must come with me now to Jerusalem," he both informed and ordered me.

"Why? Is there a war?" I asked, barely pronouncing my words.

"No," he replied. "This is an exercise to see how long it takes us to wake you guys up and get you all to Jerusalem."

"Well, if this is not a war," I concluded helpfully, "and just a practice, then practice as if I went with you, and then you'll know exactly how long it takes without my having to actually come with you."

For my part, I was only joking, really. No, really! I actually was only joking. So I went back into the house, put on my uniform, and went outside to join my unit. Outside, I noticed that he had already left. My humor was not appreciated, and it appears that the soldier took me seriously and left for Jerusalem without me. With little else to do, I resignedly went back to sleep.

The next day, I was summoned to Jerusalem to appear for trial. I guess the army hadn't looked kindly on my joking. By my not taking the drill seriously enough, perhaps a stiff sentence of a week or more in detention awaited me. I went to the trial with great apprehension.

I walked into a room with about six or seven high-ranking officers, all looking glum. They looked so serious that I almost laughed out loud. That's what happens to me when things get overly tense.

"You are aware of the charges against you," one officer solemnly declared. "Are you pleading guilty or not guilty?"

I tried to explain the story of what happened, but he would have none of it.

"Guilty or not guilty?" he sternly reiterated.

There are times when I have this uncontrollable need to pull the plug on someone's computer. Have you ever noticed that when people get into certain roles, they begin to believe in that role so much so that it seems as if you are talking to a recorded announcement? Poor is the person who believes totally in his mission. One could look at his job as play, have fun and still accomplish the same thing.

There has to be a distancing between the me and the what of what I do for a living. What I do for a living is not the total me. If it were so, I'd be completely in my ego and I would become the part rather than simply playing it. That is not fun. As George Orwell, in his short story, "Shooting an Elephant," observed of British officers in India, "They wore their masks so long that their faces grew to fit them." Well, that's what I was witnessing here: too much involvement.

How do I usually pull the plug? I do something incongruous, and unexpected. I asked a question no one would ever dare ask in a tribunal of army officers.

"Tell me, sir. What would you do in my place?"

They all looked at me in amazement. I was at least getting in touch with the human side of them, which signaled to me that the plug was halfway out.

"I'm not allowed to answer that," was his quiet reaction.

"But this is all too new to me." I persisted. "I have no experience with trials. Please tell me what you would do in my case?"

"I cannot," he repeated stiffly.

So I pulled the plug out completely.

"I feel so tense that I think I need a hug. Would you give me a hug?" I pleaded.

I do not recommend this behavior to young draftees. Take into account that I was a forty-seven year old, gray haired man, who worked as a professional educator and spoke Hebrew with an obvious American accent. A younger Israeli-born man might come off as being crass and be interpreted as exuding chutzpa. When I did it, I came off as another American loony: Loony Lenny.

"Of course, he's got to be loony. Why would an American citizen choose to live in Israel if he's not loony?" I knew they must have been thinking.

My behavior actually caused smiles. As a result, I got off with a serious reprimand instead of a jail sentence. I thanked them.

"You may leave now," one officer intoned, perfunctorily dismissing me.

I turned to them and took one last chance to make sure the plug was out and on the floor.

"I'm not leaving until I get a hug!" I persistently insisted. That did it. They completely broke up.

Again, I do not recommend to everyone this formula for unplugging overly serious people, not unless you are over forty, have an American accent, or have a rich uncle. You'll need rich relatives to pay for the plastic surgery afterward.

I served in the American Army as well, before emigrating to Israel. That experience can be just as ludicrous. I was sent to auto mechanics school immediately after basic training. Auto mechanics school? I have trouble just changing a tire! And that's the truth!

It was February in New Jersey, and that is Alaska cold. We studied in a nice, warm classroom, and I understood none of the knowledge that the instructor was trying to impart. During the break, I walked over to the instructor and asked him what would happen to those who failed the course.

"Look outside," he directed my attention.

I looked outside and saw a group of soldiers shoveling snow in the death of cold.

"That's what becomes of all those who fail this course," he promised.

I returned to my studies and I think I broke records in high grades from then on. I understood nothing, but I would be prepared to learn the telephone book by heart just not to have to go out and shovel snow.

While serving in the Israeli Reserves, I was sent to a training course for medics. Me, a medic! I can't even stand the sight of blood. I attended the courses and passed them because I claimed that I couldn't write Hebrew and requested that I do my exams in English. I knew the instructors would pass me only because they wouldn't want to bother trying to understand what I was writing.

Apparently, my trainers were so impressed with my newfound medical skills that they wound up sending me to a hospital, so that I could become a senior medic. Wow, what a joke! I still laugh out loud when I think about it. There was no way I could learn this stuff, but in the army, it doesn't matter. They give you a title, Senior Medic, and whether you know how to perform the title or not, you act the part!

It's all sort of like proclaiming, "I'm not a doctor, but I play one on TV." Try saying that in an elevator sometime and you'll be amazed at how many people only heard what they wanted to hear and wind up asking you for a ten-second diagnosis.

To prove my point: the hospital gave me a doctor's white jacket to wear. Part of the stethoscope stuck out from one of the pockets. Well, I'm sure you know what's coming. Every patient who came into the emergency ward took me for a doctor. Women approached me to tell me their most secret biological problems. It was embarrassing. Just put on a white jacket and you're in business.

One evening, they brought in a young man who had been severely injured in a motorcycle accident. He was lying on a bed with two infusions—one in each arm.

"Take this man to X-Ray!" the doctor, turning to me, ordered.

Now, in the battlefield, the wounded soldiers lie on a stretcher and the infusions are attached to the stretcher. So you pick up the stretcher along with the infusions and move the wounded soldiers out across the field, out of harm's way. In the hospital, the infusions are hooked up to the wall. Nobody bothered to tell me this! I began wheeling the bed in the direction of the X-Ray Department, when suddenly I heard two distinct "pops" behind me.

By my moving the bed, I had forced the removal of the two hooked-up infusions. Those two pops were—Oh, well!—you know what must have happened. As a result of this innocent action on my part, blood began shpritzing from his arms straight up into the air.

I heard a terrible buzzing in my ears and the room began to spin. How was I supposed to know that I was fainting? I woke up on the floor surrounded by doctors and nurses who were all shoving smelling salts capsules under my nose. I almost passed out again from the overwhelming odor of the ammonia. They had left this poor guy on the bed to bleed while they busily took care of me!

During what was proving to be Israel's many battles against Palestinian terrorists, I served in Lebanon as a medic. To have this kind of responsibility and not have the slightest idea of what I was doing was scary.

One morning, I heard the cry, "Medic!" I took for granted that that call was for me, and scurried out of my tent with my medic's bag. They brought me over to a Lebanese Phalange who had been wounded during a search. There was blood coming from his forehead. I tried to look cool, while sweat was pouring from every hole in my being.

Fake it till you make it is my motto under fire. So I reached into my bag for some kind of bandage, while this trusting Lebanese soldier waited patiently for my expert medical treatment. A crowd of Israeli soldiers huddled over me to witness my skills. I pulled out a bandage that is specifically used for stomach wounds. I was in complete confusion and tried not to show it.

"But he has a head wound. Why a stomach bandage?" one of the puzzled soldiers asked. I showed no emotion, and reacted quickly.

"I'm going to have to kneel so that I can work on this patient," I instructed. "I'm going to need padding for my knees, so the stomach bandage will do the trick."

Talk about spontaneous improvisation! The other soldiers kept offering suggestions. It seemed that they knew more than I did. I took their advice, but at one point the Phalange soldier got up, put a rag to his head and walked away in disgust!

I not only improvise these days; I actually set up a drama to unfold.

In September 1999, I decided to invite my entire family, my wife, and my three children, to spend the Jewish High Holy Days with my sister in Biloxi, Mississippi. We hadn't been together as a family for years, and were all very excited about the decision. At the end of our most wonderful vacation, and on our way back to Israel, we found ourselves stranded at the airport in Atlanta, Georgia, because of Hurricane George.

Well, that's a bit of an inconvenience, but not terrible, since we could still get back on time. My eldest son had to appear at the Habima Theater that Saturday night and I had a presentation to give that same evening. If we could catch the next day's flight out, since this was still only Thursday, all would be fine.

When we requested seats on the next day's flight, we were shocked to be informed that El Al doesn't fly on Fridays because of the political muscle behind the religious injunction against a Jewish Aircraft entering Ben Gurion Airport on the Sabbath.

Well, what about flying Saturday night and arriving Sunday, missing the performances, but at least getting home to a warm bath? We wondered among ourselves. That was also impossible because it was Yom Kippur evening, and Jewish aircraft were religiously enjoined under the same injunction not to become airborne. So what about the day after that, Sunday? Also impossible because of Yom Kippur Day itself!

The first "No!" was because of the Sabbath. The second "No!" was because of Yom Kippur Evening. The third "No!" was because of Yom Kippur Day! Frustrating, right? We were however then informed that since this hurricane was considered a natural disaster, we could transfer airline companies and have a stand-by flight with Lufthansa the following morning. This depended on one condition, though: we had to be responsible for making all the arrangements by ourselves, which, of course, spelled no end to the ensuing bureaucracy.

Now, the Atlanta airport is about the size of a city, complete with its own subway system. Hence, I was not about to start running around, wasting time and energy, trying to get permission to transfer airline companies. So I conferred with my eldest son.

"Natti," I coached, "I want you to stand between me and that lady clerk over there from the airlines and act as if you are holding me back from killing her. I'll charge at her as if I'm in a rage and you act as if you are trying to stop me, okay?"

He laughed. Natti loves improvisations, especially if it means getting a seat on the next flight out.

The plan worked splendidly without even one rehearsal. I approached the airline clerk, screaming angrily, in front of as many as one hundred people.

"You get me out of this terminal, and home! Now! Do you hear me?!" All the while, my son was holding me back.

"Take it easy, Dad," he pleaded, feigning embarrassed concern. "Don't do it! You remember what the psychiatrist said!"

The clerk coolly asked us to sit down. She later walked over to us, and as true as I'm sitting here typing on my computer, gave all of us, the whole family, not only a flight out on Lufthansa—business class, no less—but also a hotel suite for the evening!

Booking on a charter flight can also become a hassle. My wife and I once flew for a long weekend to the island of Rhodes, Greece. We spent more time in the airport than we did in the hotel in Rhodes.

Speaking of traveling: I went to Switzerland one winter to learn how to ski. I'll never do it again. All I can remember is lying on my back looking at my skis up in the air forming an "X" looming up out of the snow. It took me more than a half an hour to figure out which leg belonged to which ski, as I watched little four-year-olds swishing skillfully and effortlessly by.

These moments, at best, call for skillful and effortless improvisations. I look at all of life as an improvisation. Woe to the person who takes life too seriously. I mostly play, especially in serious circumstances, and usually have an incongruous answer for everything. My playful attitude allows me this luxury.

There was once, however, one exceptional situation where I was speechless. Can you imagine me speechless?

It happened at a time when something deep inside me made me go to the Israeli Consulate in New York City, to consider living in Israel, perhaps for the rest of my life.

I was a young actor with The New York Shakespeare Festival at the time, when a voice within me—from a source even more deeply within me than the one who had made the decision—instructed me to pack my bags and emigrate, sight unseen.

At the Israeli Embassy, I was questioned as to why I would want to make this drastic life-change.

"Do you speak Hebrew?" a clerk inquired.

"No, not a word," was my direct answer.

"Do you have friends or family in Israel?" I was asked next.

"No. I don't know a soul there," I replied.

"What is your profession?" was the next inquiry.

"I'm a Shakespearean actor," I offered. Several employees overhearing this began to chuckle.

"Why the laughter?" I inquired, turning toward the chuckling.

"You'll be a great success there," one clerk challenged, smiling. "God protects dumb, innocent people like you."

I had no spontaneous reply to this observation, perhaps because that's how I actually live. I just stay in the here and now, and believe that God will take care of the rest.

I would like to offer a parable to clarify that style of living. This parable is a pastiche, actually, of an idea inspired by Jack Canfield, *et al.'s Chicken Soup for the Soul*. I have made some adjustments of my own to suit my purpose here.

> *A gentleman by the name of Ronny was always in a good mood. He always had something positive to say to everyone.*
>
> *"The best that I can possibly be at this moment, because there is no other moment." is how he would always respond when someone asked him how he was.*
>
> *He was a unique manager and his employees always followed him around, just to be near him, because of his attitude. He was a natural motivator. If an employee were having a bad day, Ronny would tell the employee how to look at the positive side of the situation.*
>
> *Seeing this style of his made some people curious. So one day a colleague approached Ronny.*
>
> *"How can you be a positive person all of the time? How do you do it?" he quizzed him.*
>
> *Ronny replied, "Every morning I wake up with a Thank You prayer to God for the additional day of life that She/He has granted me. I then tell myself that I have two choices today. I can choose to be in a good mood or I can choose to be in a bad mood. I choose to be in a good mood. Each time that something bad happens, I can choose to be victim or I can choose to learn from it. So I choose to learn from it. Every time someone comes to me complaining, I can choose to accept their complaining or I can point out the positive side of the problem. I choose the positive side."*
>
> *"Yeah, sure, but that's not easy," protested the friend.*
>
> *"Yes it is," Ronny consoled. "Life is all about choices. When you cut away all the junk, every situation is a choice. You choose how you react to situations. You choose how people will affect your mood. You choose to be in a good*

mood or a bad mood. The bottom line is: You choose how to live every moment."

His friend reflected on what Ronny had said.

But one day, Ronny did something one must never do. He left the back door to his business open. Three men held him up at gunpoint. During the robbery, the robbers panicked and shot him. His neighbors found him and rushed him off to hospital, themselves in a panic now.

After eighteen hours of surgery and weeks of intensive care, Ronny was finally released with fragments of the bullet still in his body.

It was about a year and a half later that his colleague noticed Ronny walking about on the street again. Concerned, he asked him how he was making out these days.

"The best that I can possibly be at this moment, because there is no other moment. Would you like to see my scars?" Ronny replied joyfully.

His friend didn't care to see his scars, but instead asked him what was going on in his mind during the robbery.

"The first thing that went on in my mind was that I should have locked the back door." Ronny replied. "Then as I lay on the floor, I realized I had two choices. I could choose to live or choose to die. I chose to live."

"Weren't you scared?" interrogated the friend.

"Yes." said Ronny. "And when they wheeled me into the emergency room, and I saw that the doctors and nurses were looking at me like I was a dead man, I realized that I had to take action."

"What did you do?" asked the friend, his curiosity getting the best of him.

"Well, there was this exceptionally thin, dry nurse shouting questions at me," Ronny related. "She asked me if I were allergic to anything. I took a deep breath and yelled with all my remaining strength, 'Yes I am! I'm allergic to bullets! Especially when they come out of a gun!' I didn't

wait for them to stop laughing: so I told them, 'I have chosen to live. Please operate on me as if I'm alive, not dead.' "

Ronny lived, of course, thanks to his doctors and his remarkable attitude.

What I choose to learn from this tale of a remarkable man is that every day we have the choice to live fully in the here and now. God will take care of the rest. Attitude is everything.

What do you imagine are our choices right now?

Most people become saddened when their children leave home after college, join the army, or get married. You've heard of this reaction before, I'm sure: the Empty Nest Syndrome is what we call it. As for me, however, I felt fantastic when my kids left home.

"Now I get to use the toilet!" I joyfully exclaimed around the house. "Oh, and the telephone! I almost forgot the telephone!"

Little things about Israel that used to bother me now make me laugh. For Israelis, getting a bargain is only half the battle. The other half is paying less than one's friends do. Paying for something more than your friends or neighbors entitles you to be awarded the title of "sucker". That's the worst of shames and curses, ever since the Biblical story of Job.

Israelis intending to sign up for one of my workshops will automatically ask me for a discount without first even asking the fee.

"When is your workshop? The 14th of June? If we come as a couple, can we get a discount?"

Ask me about the registration fee first, I think to myself. Maybe it's free. And if it is, and I give you a discount to boot, then I'll end up owing you money!

Israeli men are a riot, too. I have noticed that when an Israeli man walks, his crotch gets to his destination three centimeters ahead of the rest of his body. That's because of the amount of testosterone that is rampant in Israeli men.

I pay attention when they walk. Their testicles clang. Every step they take is accompanied by a knocking sound. This, again, is due to the abundance of the male hormone testosterone that Israeli men are blessed with. When they are talking on the phone, they never leave that particular place down there alone for one minute.

"How's it goin', brother?" they ask into the phone—and then tug at their pants below the belt.

"Not bad. How's it with you?"—another tug.

I believe that humor, optimism, laughter, and love are universal and that we don't need to know another's language to speak it. The grammar of joy is all we need.

Once, as I was riding on a packed elevator in Cairo, Egypt, a small, cheery, bald-headed Egyptian waiter got on with a tray. Don't ask me why, but when he looked at me, and I looked at him, we both started laughing hilariously. We couldn't stop. I opened my arms, he put his tray down, opened his, and we hugged and laughed. When the elevator arrived at his floor, he picked up his tray and left the elevator still laughing. I never saw him again. I wonder if he thinks of me once in a while.

I love to see the human side of people. While in a restaurant, a very busy waiter approached and asked what we wanted to order. I detected a Spanish accent, and asked him if he spoke Spanish. He said that he did. I told him that I spoke Spanish, too, which I don't. So he spoke some Spanish to me. I answered him in Spanish gibberish. He laughed out loud. We connected. Every time he passed our table, he smiled and touched my shoulder. Human contact. Even for a moment. How much we all need this!

This very same scene took place in an Italian Restaurant, but the waiter, rather than seeing the joke, asked me if I were from Southern Italy! Perhaps he had trouble understanding my accent.

Like everything else, humor, laughter, and acts of kindness cause a chain reaction. I travel to New York once a year for study and fun. I make up my mind, even before boarding the plane, that I will choose never to be disappointed with what will eventually happen once I get there. My goal is to learn from all that occurs, and to spread laughter and love at every opportunity, knowing that what I project onto the Cosmos, will eventually come back to me.

One evening, I was on the New York subway system. Anyone who knows anything about New York City subways is also familiar with the lack of human contact that goes on there. People will not look into your eyes, smile, or offer any recognition. The atmosphere is one of fear. Travelers will stare at the advertisements on the walls, read the newspaper, or gaze at the floor. They will do anything to avoid connecting to one another.

Suddenly, a slim, young black man entered our coach. He was shouting out things. He seemed not to be making sense, and this annoyed and frightened everyone, myself included. Remembering that my existence entails love and laughter, I decided to listen intently to what he was raving about.

"When Ah was growin' up, we was so po', my momma would take us kids to Kentucky Fried Chicken so's we could lick da' fingahs of da' otha' folk," he revealed.

I began to smile and listen further.

"My momma, she went to da' movies one day. Da' sign said, 'No one under eighteen allowed.' So she went home and got seventeen mo' folks to go wiff huh."

I cracked up. It was obvious that the other passengers had no idea how to handle this. Some started smiling in disbelief when I complimented the young man.

"Hey, you are good!" I beamed appreciatively. "Here, take this five dollars!" I knew instinctively that his show ought to be awarded with a small offering.

"Naw,!" he refused. "I don't take no money."

I was quite surprised until I looked over to my right and saw two policemen standing near the exit. I understood, then, the danger this man might be in by accepting my monetary gratitude. I looked over at one of the policemen and smiled.

"I'm giving him a loan, officer. He promised to pay me back tomorrow!" They both turned to me.

"What about me? Don't I get a loan?" one of the officers suggested.

At this, I witnessed, for the first time in my life, an entire subway car roaring with laughter. A moment of humanity on the New York

City Subway System: American history was in the making!

Whenever I walk along the streets of any city, I try to be sensitive to the homeless, or to any other person who is looking for a handout. I feel that God has been so generous with me that I consider it a missed opportunity when I am unable or unprepared to give something to someone who asks me for something. Whenever I give, I receive a blessing from that person in whatever language they speak. Sometimes we might have a short conversation.

"Here's five dollars, friend. Have a nice day," I once said to an apparent homeless person.

"Hey, buddy!" he shot back. "Give me ten and I'll get off the streets forever! I promise!"

We both had a good laugh.

Laughter, humor, and love know no language barrier. In the 1960s, my wife, pregnant with our second son, and I were living in Birmingham, Alabama. My wife, surely because she is Middle Eastern from birth, has always loved Arabic food, but as my wife entered her seventh month, love turned to craving! And crave she did—all of it: humus, tahina, tabouleh, labna, pita bread, and on and on. Well, we had a real problem on our hands, because the closest thing to Arabic food in Birmingham was a MacDonald's.

My wife's eyes widened as she exclaimed, "Ahhh! I know a fabulous Arab restaurant!" I leapt to my feet in excitement!

"Where is it? What's the name of the place? I'll go there right away!"

"It's called Omar El Khayam and it's in Pittsburgh," she declared, staring at me piercingly. "Quick! Call them and order some food!"

"Pittsburgh? As in Pennsylvania?" I beamed back.

"Yes! Yes!" she yelled. "Call them right now. Oh, I have such a craving!"

I tried to explain to her that Pittsburgh was over 1,000 miles north of Birmingham, and it would be impossible to get the food to satisfy her craving. Well, she would hear nothing of such drivel.

"Call them, now!" she demanded. "Call them and order the stuff and tell them to bring it by plane!" she cried. "Now!"

Seeing my wife unhappy is no easy thing for me; so I called the restaurant long distance and placed the order with the owner. When I gave him the address where to send it, there was silence.

"Are you joking?" barked the restauranteur from the other side.

"No, you see, my wife is pregnant and craves your food. She ate at your place once and can't forget it. Can you go to the airport in Pittsburgh and give the order to someone who is traveling to Birmingham, and we'll meet him at the airport here and send you the money by bank check?" I stammered out breathlessly.

There was silence.

"Sir, I am an Arab," he informed me proudly. "I was born in Syria. If I come to the airport with a package to give someone to take on any flight, I'm looking at thirty years in prison. Airport security does not look generously upon Arabs bearing packages at airports. Let me talk to your wife."

I handed her the phone. She told him she was Israeli. He patiently explained that he, too, has a wife who is pregnant and he understood, and that if we are ever in Pittsburgh, to come and eat on the house. She smiled and relaxed because of his patience, understanding, empathy, and good will. Imagine that! A Syrian and an Israeli in confluence!

Another instance involving a cross culture misunderstanding was trying to explain Halloween to my wife.

"Tonight is Halloween. Kids, celebrating the holiday by dressing in outrageous costumes, will be coming to the door constantly throughout the evening, ringing the doorbell and shouting "Trick or Treat!"

"You smile back," I explained "and give them some candy, or else they will trick you."

She seemed to like that old American custom. We went out and bought a ton of candies, fruits, gum, and nuts. That evening I was in the shower when the doorbell rang. I yelled to my wife to get it. When I came out of the shower, and went into the kitchen, I noticed something very strange. All the candies, nuts, fruits and gum were gone.

"Where's all the stuff I bought?" I asked in panic.

"I gave it to the kid, like you told me," she answered innocently.

Suddenly there was another doorbell ring. Obviously, others, ecstatic, had heard of the big tipper from the East and were coming in droves.

"Didn't I explain that they would be coming all night? Not just one kid. Hundreds. That's the custom!" I cried. "What are we going to do now?"

"Let me handle it," she coolly responded. She walked to the door with one stick of gum and began tearing it up into small pieces, dropping each piece into the open bags the children were holding. She then turned to me and smiled.

"I have more gum. I'll keep doing this until you come back from the store with another batch." She patted the children on their heads and closed the door. As I was hurriedly leaving to make the second purchase, there was another ring at the door.

"Quickly! I don't know how much longer this gum will last!" she laughed.

It takes courage to be spontaneous and do what we sometimes fantasize doing. The fear is, *What will people think of me?* That's a very normal fear since we all want to be loved and are deathly afraid of rejection. But what I have discovered is that when I put my fear aside and do something really crazy, I am at such times exuding that same madness that makes others feel closer to me, and me to them.

For example, I never wait in line at the post office. When I see a long line, I usually walk around to the back of the building to ring the red button. Only post office employees are allowed to use this red button. They ring it to summon one of the clerks to open the door to receive packages.

I really push hard on the button, which makes a very loud clang. When one of the clerks opens the door, and before he or she can, after seeing it's only me (again), and slam the door shut again, I force myself in, fall on my knees, and beg, "Please, please, please!" This always gets me a smile, and my letters and packages, without ever having to wait in line!

When I order a taxi by phone, I try not to get sucked into little agitations.

"Is this is the taxi company?" I call and ask.

The answer is usually a matter-of-fact "Yes."

Then the crazy making begins.

"I'd like to order a taxi—" I begin.

"Wait a minute!"

I'm cut off as he answers another phone. Eventually, he comes back.

"What do you want, sir?"

"I'd like to—" I say once again, but again I'm cut off, as he again tends to something else!

He comes back. "What do you want, sir?"

"I'd like two pizzas with mushrooms to go," I say to battle this madness.

"What?" comes the shocked reply?

Now I've got him on the other side of the stick, and am going to make him crazy.

"I want two pizzas to go!" I repeat, this time with a hint of exasperation in my voice.

"What?" I hear again?

"Isn't this the pizza shop?" I ask impatiently.

"No," comes the stunned answer.

"Then send a taxi to 307 Roy Street immediately, please," I shout into the phone.

It gets them every time.

When it comes to being overcome by madness, I do have one regret. I was a student at Emerson College in Boston, back in the mid 1950s. The Metropolitan Opera had come to town with a production of Verdi's Othello and a casting call had gone out for students to play the silent soldiers—no dialogue—in the show. The pay was only one dollar per performance but it offered up the once in a lifetime opportunity to be on stage alongside the great tenor, Mario Del Monaco, and the grandest of all baritones, Leonard Warren.

We were about twenty soldiers, mostly students, and we needed only one rehearsal an hour before curtain. The stage manager practiced us a few times in running across the stage, as if in an attack. Then it hit me! What would happen if I were to run across the stage, and at one point, stop, go to the edge of the stage, look out into the vast audience, and let out one, piercing operatic note at the top of my lungs, and run back off stage.

"Yes!" I informed myself! I would do it! What's the worst thing that could happen? I'd get arrested for singing an operatic note? How would they determine my sentence or fine?

I gathered all the actor-soldiers together and told them of my plan, on one condition. They were all to give me the one-dollar that they were to have earned after I had pulled this thing off. They all agreed with great excitement and laughter. Why not allow someone to do something crazy once in a while and make a little money at it? Twenty dollars in those days were worth three weeks of rent.

The most respected opera singers in the entire world were in place just before the curtain. The audience was packed with Boston's richest, most prominent citizens. Then came the hush as the house lights went out.

"I'm going to do it," I coaxed myself, as electricity seemed to snap all over my chest and stomach.

Then the enormous choir joined in as the curtain rose and a loud, roaring applause was heard from the standing room only audience. I never thought that the choir was going to be this huge and forceful. Even if I had screamed with all my might, I would never have been heard. The floor under me was rocking from the vibrations emanating from the choir and orchestra pit. Then as the soldiers got ready to run across the stage, they looked at me, smiled, and gave me the thumbs-up sign. I ran with them, stopped, turned to the audience as planned, took two steps toward the black void, looked out, opened my arms, took a deep breath, and in a split second, found myself running back to join the fold.

I didn't do it! I couldn't do it.

Backstage, the student actors called me chicken shit. I didn't answer. They were right. To this day, I regret that I missed the one moment of madness that I could have told my grandchildren about.

During my time as an actor, I thought that I had a pretty decent singing voice. However, the most commonly heard word, immediately after I'd finish my audition for a musical, was "Next!" I had painstakingly rehearsed the ballad, "On The Street Where You Live" from the musical, *My Fair Lady*.

The song begins with the words, "I have often walked on this street before . . ."; and I never got past the word "before" when I would hear a resounding, "Next!" coming from the darkened auditorium. I got fed up with this and blamed my lack of success on the material. Instead, I decided to rehearse the song, "Love is a Many Splendored Thing," knowing that the bravado ending would land me many a job for sure.

I got ready for my first audition with this piece by pumping myself up with confidence and positive self-talk.

"I'm the man! I'm the greatest! I'm the Dude! The greatest!"

I was surprised at my own behavior when I strutted into this one particular audition as I was the world's greatest gift to Broadway. When the director asked me to stand near the microphone, I was shocked to hear myself say, with tremendous self-assurance, "I never use a microphone."

At this point, the jaded pianist accompanying the singers sat straight up and played me a million-dollar introduction. Even the janitor dropped his broom and came closer to witness the world's next Caruso. I opened my arms and let out the worst note off key ever witnessed in the history of modern music. And then I heard the familiar "Next!"

Today, my eldest son is a well-known actor in Israel. His first big professional break was in a revival of a production of the musical Hair. The director ordered all the male actors to grow their hair as long as possible to recreate the hippy scene of the 1960s. My son, however, decided to get a haircut instead.

He called me later to tell me how the director was beside himself with frenzy and almost threw him out of the production for this.

"Natti," I suggested patiently, "it's a good thing that the name of the play isn't 'Dick.'"

I believe I began teaching humor at my institute as a corrective experience. In my courses, we learn a type of humor used to cope with little irritations. I call it Aikido Humor, improvising on the martial arts by that name. The main point is to take a negative remark such as some humiliation or joke intended to shame, and then to use the attacker's offense to your own advantage.

One woman once offered a good example by way of posing a question to the humor class.

"My baby fell off the bed and hurt herself. My maid said, 'How come that always happens to you? It never happens to me.' How can I handle this? She does the same when I burn the food or drop the telephone by mistake."

The humor class helped her by suggesting that if the baby falls off the bed again and the maid once again says, "Why does that always happen to you?", she should then respond to her by saying, "Boy, I'm glad it worked this time. Do you know how many times we rehearsed her falling off the bed until she got it right?"

One man asked the humor class for help by offering, "I'm a teacher. Whenever I give homework to my class, they complain by saying that I'm not fair, or I'm too hard on them. They moan and groan and complain. This makes me feel that maybe I am too difficult with them and perhaps I am unfair."

The humor class came up with the following: "Enter class with a menu. On the menu will appear all the complaints that they usually have when you give homework. Tell them you would like them to choose their favorite complaint-of-the-day. Ask them, 'Who would like to choose, You're too difficult? And who would like to choose, You're not fair? Please raise your hands first. This way you get the complaints out of the way from the beginning. Afterwards say, 'Thank you for choosing your favorite complaint-of-the-day. And now here's the homework for tonight.'"

The courses, workshops, and seminars that I offer in Gestalt Psychotherapy and humor are literally hands-on. I offer some theory but most of the time is spent on the experiential and the practical. There are academics that study the theory of humor and laughter. They are considered the serious researchers and are given much respect in the academic world. One woman heard me give a funny keynote address in Holland in February of 2000, and had this observation: "I listened to all the academics and their theory on the subject of humor and laughter. They gave me the menu and expected me to eat it. You served the food."

One woman who had come to my weekend humor workshop actually passed out from laughing. Her head became as heavy as a rock as she fell into my arms.

"Put her legs up!" someone in the group shouted.

Of course, I should have known. I used to be a battlefield medic. Remember? I lifted her legs up as her eyes disappeared into her forehead. Her skin turned white as I turned to the group to announce, "When you leave this workshop, remember to tell your family and friends that you attended a humor workshop where a woman actually died laughing."

At that the group started laughing, and the woman who had fainted from laughter, began laughing again. Her eyes snapped back into place, and color returned to her skin as she continued to choose Life through laughter.

A couple left at the end my weekend workshop, and were caught speeding on the way home. As the policeman asked them to role down their window, they roared with laughter, still reeling from the effects of the workshop. The policeman, quite shocked, asked them what was so funny.

"You are the cutest officer we have ever seen," the woman chuckled.

"Nobody's ever told me that before," the policeman blushed, as he let them go.

One person who came to see me was an elderly woman who had suffered for years from the aftereffects of the Holocaust. I offered her an experiment. I asked her to recreate the death camp in her imagination, to look at the Nazis, and to try laughing out loud. It was difficult at first, but she succeeded. During her bursts of laughter, she added, "You didn't kill me. You failed. I'm alive!"

I would like to end this chapter with a few thoughts on finding the blessings, optimism, humor, and miracles in our lives. Can anyone define what a blessing is and what a curse is? Sometimes we can't, and declare, "You never know." Here's a story about *You Never Know*.

> *There once was a farmer who had a lovely pony. One day the pony escaped the barn and ran away.*
>
> *"That's terrible luck," said his neighbors.*
>
> *"You never know," proclaimed the farmer.*
>
> *The next day, the pony came back, followed by a handsome black stallion.*
>
> *"What great luck," said his neighbors.*
>
> *"You never know," said the farmer.*
>
> *The farmer's son tried riding the stallion fell off and broke his leg.*
>
> *"Tough luck," frowned his neighbors.*
>
> *"You never know," repeated the farmer.*
>
> *A war broke out and all the young, able men were drafted into the army. They did not take the farmer's son, since he was considered an invalid.*
>
> *"You are a lucky father," beamed his neighbors.*
>
> *So what did the farmer say? Of course, he said, "You never know!"*

When someone asks me what I do for a living, I reply, "I don't really know." I really don't! This response drives taxi drivers nuts.

Should I have learned the lesson from *The Book of Life* that Anonymous did not seem to learn either: "I always wanted to be Somebody. I think I should have been more specific!"?

CHAPTER TWELVE

Endless Optimism

*Optimists do better in school, win more elections, and
succeed more at work than pessimists do.*
            —Martin E.P. Seligman

Endless optimism means knowing that all we are doing at every
moment, including this one, is following choice. All that has
happened to us up to this time has been the journey we had to take
to learn, to grow, and to love so that we could be where we are and
become who we are at this point in time.

We all have been guided by our inner being, if we would just take
the time to feel and listen carefully to this being. That inner being of
ours has guided us to all the coincidences and mistakes we had to
experience, to finish the business we had to complete so that we
could continue to our next stage of spiritual growth.

Equally important is being capable of accepting the fact that we
are all valuable and deserving beings. To be optimists, we must
always picture in our mind the best that life has to offer. By doing just
that, we invite the best into our life.

What we project, we inject. Every successful life requires both the
accurate appreciation of reality and the ability to dream beyond the
present reality. As Janet Stanfield sings, "I'm not lost, I am exploring."

Does the fact that there are no mistakes and coincidences mean that we have actually chosen and continue to choose those poisonous relationships, divorces, abandonments, rejections and illnesses? My answer is, "Yes." Once we take responsibility for having chosen them, and then choose to learn and grow from our choices, we are scraping the edge of the meaning of life. But where's the optimism and humor in that?

In my past, I chose very poisonous relationships. Most of my friends, business partners, and people who worked with and for me were critical, judgmental, and destructive. When I took ownership of these choices I had made, and realized that I had invited these relationships into my life to clean up unfinished businesses of my past, in order to move on and to grow, my life changed radically.

I once approached a married couple that I had been close to for about twenty years. This couple would use every available opportunity to lower my self-esteem and chip away at my self-confidence. There wasn't an evening I spent with them that I didn't come home with a headache. And still, I continued seeing them week after treacherous week.

Finally, I actually thanked them for playing the part I had cast them into.

"I guess I need your poison in order to learn and grow," I explained to them one evening. "Otherwise, why would I have invited you into my life? I suppose that when I stop needing this poisonous relationship, and learn what I have to learn from it, I'll be able to say goodbye to you. In the meantime, thanks."

They smiled at this and I laughed.

There is often a lot of humor in the truth. By not blaming them, but rather by taking responsibility for my own choices, I was eventually able to finish that relationship and seek out more positive ones.

If, in the event I choose other harmful relationships in the future, I will remind myself, "I guess I haven't learned what I have to learn. If I had, I would be choosing more nourishing relationships."

How long does it take for a lesson to be learned? A week? A day? A year? What happens after the lesson is learned? When do we find the humor in it?

I opened a business some years back with a partner, since I really hadn't the confidence to do it all alone. I chose a very competent, loving, but very critical and enraged person to be my partner. Our relationship had been torrential at times and quite painful. We were together for nine years.

Nine years of fear, sadness, love, and criticisms, with a lot of harm being done to both of us.

Only when I could accept the fact that I had chosen him and he had chosen me, in order to work out old, unfinished businesses from the past, and only when I could accept the part of him in my own personality that I was hiding from myself, and projecting on to him, could we finally separate.

We finally parted as stormily as we had related in the past: lawyers, attempted lawsuits, bad-mouthing each other to other people, as if the previous nine years had not bestowed a good day between us. But there had been wonderful things that had gone on between us. We just refused to recognize them. When we ended the relationship in 1995, it was without goodbyes, or even a hug. From the moment he left for America, there was neither word nor letter nor telephone from either of us.

I grew in light years professionally as well as emotionally as a result of this loving, painful relationship. While attending a Self Esteem Seminar in Santa Barbara, California, in July of 2000, I was given—as if by the grace of God—the opportunity to finish my business with my former partner.

The participants at the seminar were requested to couple up in order to undertake a process that would allow each of us to create for ourselves the appreciation we needed from a significant other from our past. My former partner's image suddenly came to mind. I used the good services of the person I had coupled up with to get the appreciation from my former partner that I had failed to get when we had shared a friendship and a business together. When I finally completed the appreciation segment of the process, I felt overwhelmed and at the same time, satisfied. I had gotten the appreciation that I had needed, even if the one I had completed it with wasn't there.

When I got home from the seminar, I checked my e-mail. I couldn't believe it! There on the computer screen before me was a personal message from my former partner asking that we forget the bad times, remember the good times, and resume communicating with each other. It was a request for forgiveness. I noted the date of the letter and time. He had composed his request to renew our friendship the same day and time I had completed the appreciation process at the seminar in Santa Barbara.

A very weird experience, wouldn't you say?

So how long does it take to finish a cycle of unfinished business? In this case, it took us almost fifteen years. Where is the humor in this? We both now laugh and smile when we talk to each other on the phone. We will continue to laugh and smile when we meet in the future, knowing that we have cared for our souls and bodies over the years apart. We forgave each other and chose love. Carrying around old angers can cause terrible damage, both physically and mentally.

After I accepted to learn this lesson, I blessed him silently for having accepted my invitation to play a very significant part in my life. At this point in time, I choose to open my heart to people. I have also become an inverted paranoid.

An inverted paranoid is one who chooses to believe that people are saying good things about him behind his back. It works. When you expect to get loving energy from people, they will most often give you what you expect. The truth is also in reverse, of course.

Whenever I have difficulties with someone, I usually take responsibility for recognizing the difficulties and ask myself, "*What did I project on to this person in order to get a negative response from him?*" I have found that by smiling more at people, I become the receiver of a lot more smiles. By loving and laughing, I become the receiver of much more love and laughter.

Endless optimism means knowing that everything will work out in the end. I've lived through several wars in Israel. During the Six-Day War, I had been living in Elat, Israel's most southern town on the Red Sea, with my wife and six-month-old son. When the sirens went off, everyone headed for the shelters. My wife ran out of the house to the shelter, yelling back at me, "Take the baby!"

I quickly wrapped up in the blanket what I had thought was my infant son and headed toward the shelter. When I got there, I unwrapped the blanket only to realize that what I had taken with me, in my haste and panic, was the radio.

You have to have optimism in cases such as these.

When the sirens went off on another occasion, during the same war, a woman approached me while we were safe in our shelter and begged me to please fetch her father from the fourth floor and bring him to the shelter. He was old and needed help. I left the shelter, ran up to the fourth floor, and found a seriously ill old man, who had every conceivable sickness known to mankind. He shook and could barely walk. I was quite anxious and frightened, not knowing what would befall us.

Each step down the stairs took about ten minutes to maneuver. By the time we reached the last step, the siren was blasting the all clear. Every one was headed back home by this time; so it was slowly up the stairs again in an attempt to get this old man back to his abode. I prayed that another siren would not sound, at least not now, as I helped him back to his apartment.

Boy, was I being optimistic!

During the scud missile attacks in the war with Iraq named Desert Storm, a siren would go off, encouraging the citizens to put on their gas masks. My wife never learned to wear her gas mask properly, and always had a trace of fog on the plastic area around her eyes. She tried to talk on the phone with her gas mask on, in muffled tones, attempting to get information as to the welfare of our children, who lived away from home.

One could hardly decipher what she was trying to say while yelling through her gas mask. I once figured that I might as well add to the absurdity of such a moment and proceeded, as well, to force a kiss on her with my mask still on. A mask to mask kiss, you might say. I still remember it, as if it were yesterday, her laughter as she shouted, in muffled tones, behind her mask, "What are you doing? Are you crazy?"

"No, my dear. Just endlessly optimistic," I replied lustily.

I would like to, if I may, walk you through just one positive, optimistic day.

It was Valentine's Day, 2001. This had been my second invitation to come to Holland to present a workshop on Humor and Optimism. As is my usual habit, I arrived two days early, to rest, to kick back and just hang out. I had the day to myself, and whenever I'm in a foreign country, I like to have lots of time to walk around, observe, do nothing, and let God bring to me what the here and now has to offer.

My Buddha Walk brought me to a lovely shopping center where I decided to check out, and perhaps buy, a nice stylish hat for myself. I had in mind what I wanted. Upon entering a haberdashery, I spotted my dream hat, tried it on, and found that it suited me perfectly. I recognized instantly that it was me!

The storeowner also approved.

"Do you like that hat?" he inquired. "It's Italian. It looks very nice on you."

I asked this stranger whether he believed in God. He smiled when I told him that God led me to his store to get exactly what I wanted.

"You are a very lucky man," he informed me, as he put my handsome purchase into a bag.

"Yes I am," I agreed, as I left the store. "God is forever sending me to places to get exactly what I need."

We shared a smile as I walked away.

As I left his store, and went out onto the street, I suddenly remembered that I needed an after-shave. I found a store with a very cute, young sales girl. She asked me what kind of shaving lotion I had in mind.

"Something that would attract a beautiful young girl like you," I confessed, "to a rather mature gentleman like myself." Then I added, "Not that I'd be able to do anything once the attraction—"

She didn't miss a beat and was behind the counter fetching me the after-shave of her choice. I asked her to wrap it up for me.

"Don't you even want to smell it first?" She questioned.

I smiled, "If you like it, I don't have to test it."

She blushed," Yes, I like it."

I looked squarely at her and laughed.

"It's Valentine's Day. You can tell me you love me, for God's sakes!",

"No, I don't think so!" she replied assertively.

As I turned to walk out, she blurted, "How about something for your lady."

"I bought something for her already," I smiled.

"Did she like it?"

"I haven't given it to her yet."

"I hope she likes it."

"She will."

"How do you know?"

"It's from me. She'll love anything as long as it's from me."

Now that's optimism!

After that lovely confrontation, I decided to take a bus to Volendam, a Dutch fishing village. Someone back home suggested that I would enjoy it, and I never go against God's command. If it is to pleasure me, then God has something to do with it, I believe.

While waiting for the bus to my destination, I noticed a group of teen-agers standing around the depot. For some reason, one thirteen- or fourteen-year-old boy was staring at me. I smiled. He made a grimace. I grimaced back, and our three-minute dialogue consisted of making faces at each other, interfused with smiles and laughter. Then he uttered a word as if to ask me a question, while pointing straight at me.

"Homo?"

I didn't know what language to answer him in; so I shrugged my shoulders, to communicate, "I don't really know."

I laughed out loud at his reaction, which was a smile imbued with a certain disbelieving. He was probably thinking, "This guy is nuts."

My outburst of laughter caused the crowd at this Amsterdam bus terminal to gaze blankly at me. As I boarded my bus, I waved goodbye to the young fellow, who waved and smiled back.

These small, yet unforgettable moments are nothing short of miracles to me. They contain no words, and yet for me, they are infused with a deep human dialogue between perfect strangers.

Humor, a smile and some laughter, know no age boundaries.

In Volendam, a gray, chilly, drizzly day greeted me as I approached the sea. The salty breeze and cold air brought back memories of my childhood and my strolls along the Atlantic Ocean. A middle-aged man approached me and spoke to me in Dutch. I answered him in English and he quickly switched to a fluent, accented English.

"If you are hungry, I can recommend my restaurant, which will certainly satisfy your appetite," he offered.

I followed him, and he soon ushered me into his cozy nook about the size of a small bedroom. There were seats for only four people. On display were all types of raw fish.

"Have you ever eaten eel?" he asked with a smile.

"No," I answered. "And that's all the reason I need to try it."

He cut open the eel, put chopped, raw onions on it and handed it to me.

"Do you have some bread? I asked.

"No, but you can buy some there, at my sister's place," he indicated, pointing to an adjacent bakery.

"And a beer?" I inquired.

"No, but my brother's place is not to far from here."

"You have a large family working this beat," I said, looking up at him from my seat.

He laughed, remarking, "Oh, yes. Every one in the village is my family. We call each other brother and sister since we grew up together and our families go way back."

I tasted the eel and devoured it with passion.

I ordered a herring, and he prepared it as he narrated the fate of his village a few years back.

"This village was almost completely destroyed by fire. Fifty-five of my brothers and sisters died. There are fifty of my children still crippled." Then he came from around the counter carrying the raw herring.

"A team of very famous soccer players volunteered to play a game to donate money to our children. To make life easier for them."

I believed I detected that he had become teary-eyed, as he remembered the acts of kindness and of love of others that he so proudly related to me.

I thought a lot about that encounter as I was driven back to Amsterdam. I walked through town with a map, to try to find my way back to my hotel. I had no idea where I was. I stopped two policewomen to ask directions. One of them spotted the map I was carrying.

"Why do you ask directions when you have a map? Don't you know how to read a map?" one blurted.

"Yes, I do," I came back. "But it's Valentines Day, and how else am I going to have a chance to talk to two pretty ladies."

They laughed and gave instructions.

I can never forget these instances and opportunities that life has to offer.

As I approached my hotel, I came upon a hot dog vendor. I ordered a hot dog, the likes of which I hadn't eaten since I was a small boy. It was a huge hot dog, with mustard, relish and raw onions. I bit into it, heard it crackle in my mouth, and tasted a wave of delight as the memories of the baseball games I had attended as a kid flashed by. I could actually hear the sound of the bat against the ball in midair, confirming a solid hit, the unified shout from the crowd as I watched, in my mind's eye, as the ball soared up and out of the stadium. I took a second bite and closed my eyes.

That was Valentine's Day in Amsterdam. I meditated on the thought that If we just let things happen and accept God's unexpected gifts of the moment, and let go of the need to control what happens in the here and now, we can learn to be optimistic. Sometimes we need to let things happen, rather than make them happen.

I thought of home, Israel, and of the tension and hatred between two peoples struggling for existence there. I tried to imagine my turning on the television in my hotel room, watching the news, and witnessing Israeli soldiers handing out flowers and chocolates to the Palestinian stone throwers of the Intifada. I realize that no government would ever issue that kind of order, but that couldn't stop me from daydreaming.

I do believe that peace in the Middle East will be achieved neither through war nor through statesmanship. Peace will come when just one Israeli, who is committed to love and understanding, raises his or her hand to clasp the hand of the one Palestinian prepared to live in peace and harmony. When this happens, I truly believe others will dare to join hands and form a bond of loving energy. This is a marvelous option in combating terror.

Terror needs an opposition. The opposite of terror is love. Terror fuels more terror. Love invites love.

I am sixty-four years old. If I stay in bed doing nothing for the rest of the year, I'll sooner or later be sixty-five. Anyone can get older. That doesn't take any talent or ability. The idea is to grow up finding opportunities for change. I have no regrets for what I have done. I can only regret the things I didn't do.

My advice to everyone is to find humor and laughter in every day life. We do not stop laughing because we've grown old. We grow old because we've stopped laughing. So let's have dreams. When we lose our dreams, we die. So many people are walking around dead and don't know it. Growing older is mandatory. Growing up is optional. It's never too late to be all that we can possibly be.

Live life, my dear readers, but don't become attached to it. It's a temporary gift. Choose love over fear. The opposite of love is not hate. It's fear. Look upon the world with love, laughter, humor, and optimism-and all of it will be returned to you in abundance.

Ram Dass has observed: "Behind the machinations of our brilliant, undependable minds is an essence that is not conditional, a being that aging does not alter, to which nothing can be added, from which nothing is taken away. The more we become aware of this being, which is our Soul and the source of our strength, the less we will be prey to the illusion of meaninglessness."

I encourage everyone to follow his or her own heart. Doing

something without having our hearts in it is not worth doing. We must do what we truly love and be paid handsomely for it. Some people think it's a crime to love what we do and do what we love, and also be paid for it.

There is no other way, however. Consider the inverse: doing something we don't like just for the money will invariably lead to sickness and depression.

When we do something from the heart, we can be sure that God's hand is in it. This will attract money, fame, love, health, humor, laughter, and all the good things that we deserve. We came into this world to have fun, to laugh, to love, and to learn. All the rest is technical. If it's not turning out exactly that way, stop and ask yourself, "*What am I doing to prevent joy, love and laughter in my life?*" Then, write a new script and reap all the good stuff that life has to offer. It's magic.

Challenges and difficulties are all part of the game. There are no ups and downs. There is only *That Which Is*. And we can drag it or we can dance it. That's why I choose to be endlessly optimistic. I love to dance. Especially Life!

I like to stare in the mirror for some length of time, on occasion, and fall in love, over and over and over again. While I do this, I think to myself, "*I am perfect. Everything is perfect at this moment. I have all that I have ever wanted. All that I have ever dreamed of has come true. All that I choose to dream of in the future shall also come true. Thank you, God.*"

Shall we dance?

For more information on Lenny Ravich, you may visit his website at http://www.LennyRavich.com.

For further information on the Gestalt Institute of New Orleans/
Metairie, visit their website at http://www.Teachworth.com.

Other publications of the Gestalt Institute Press available through Xlibris are:
WHY WE PICK THE MATES WE DO, by Anne Teachworth and
THOSE WHO COME AFTER, by Renate Perls with Eileen J. Ain, Ph.D.

The Gestalt Institute of New Orleans, Inc.
1539 Metairie Road
Metairie, Louisiana 70005
USA
1-800-GESTALT
1-504-828-2267 (Outside USA)